Think

Applying the Success
Principles of 1918 Today

By

COL. WM. C. HUNTER

GetSwitchedOn.com
Knoxville, TN

Chuck -
Enjoy this
classic

Chip

To my Granny

Get Switched On!
745 Bowman Bend Road
Harriman, TN 37748

Chip Eichelberger
Chip@GetSwitchedOn.com

866-224-1393

Cover Design: Andrew Theo - Creative Design & Development Inc.

ISBN 1-59975-706-0

— ORIGINAL PUBLISHER'S NOTE — from 1918

When Colonel Hunter wrote PEP in 1914 and offered it to The Reilly & Britton Company, we immediately accepted the manuscript for publication. So highly did we regard the work that the president of this company, over his signature, contributed an introductory note of endorsement, citing his own experience in following the rules and principles laid down in PEP for the attainment of "poise, efficiency and peace."

Our confidence and belief in PEP were amply justified. Eight large editions were printed in four years. Over 70,000 copies have been sold.

THINK — the last book that Colonel Hunter wrote — is now published for the first time. It is especially important, coming, as it does, at a time when commonsense thinking, good health, good cheer, optimism and rational methods of living are more necessary than ever before.

In this trenchantly written volume, Colonel Hunter has given some golden advice to the man or woman who is facing the big problems of to-day in a wavering or hopeless spirit. Correct your thinking. Get a grip on yourself. Colonel Hunter tells you how.

INTRODUCTION

My Granny, Grace Patterson was an amazing woman in many ways and the only Grandparent I ever had the chance to really know. Always full of spunk and an opinion to share, she was the one who started me reading personal development books. My favorite one we would read together was this book. It has been almost ten years since she passed away and I have had it on my shelf since then. It is my favorite memento from her.

Frequently I would quote from it on stage to my audiences to contrast the thinking in 1918 to today. As you will read, you will be surprised by Col. Hunter's opinions about: the changes in their modern life, charity, the placebo effect, the pill fiend, religion, the pursuit of wealth and the perils of inactivity just to name a few. Check out chapter 32 right now if you want to be really amazed that it was much more modern in 1918 than you had imagined!

How did this edition come to be? My good friend Scott deMoulin gave me a classic book our friend and mentor Bob Procter had reprinted called *The Science of Getting Rich* from Wallace Wattles written in 1912. Until then I did not know that books written before 1923 were in the public domain and I could publish **Think** myself. I did a little research and found it was not uncommon to do.

This book was originally intended to be read in the evenings for fifteen minutes a day with the goal of getting you to think! This is how Col. Hunter puts it:

"I want to help YOU to form the habit of thinking over each day's activities in the quiet, relaxed, uncolored, unprejudiced, secluded environment of your home. Are you getting the best out of yourself? Or are you plodding along aimlessly, scattering your energy in a haphazard, hit-or-miss fashion that benefits nobody? Are you growing or standing still?"
Think, Col Wm. C. Hunter

You may have to pull out the dictionary occasionally, I did. I helped you in several cases by putting the definition in parentheses for you. For example, one of my favorite words in the book and one very common back then is **pluck:**

The trait of showing courage and determination in spite of possible loss or injury.

Also, spelling on some words has changed over time. If you see something that doesn't look correct that is probably it. I have reprinted the book exactly as it was written. The examples about working and career are typically all male. Remember, the book was written before women were given the right to vote in 1920. There are many touching areas about daughters, women, wives and mothers in the book as you will read. You will not agree with everything in the book of course and it is an amazing collection of wisdom, which is as applicable today as almost 100 years ago.

Share the book with your family, children and colleagues. This book is available in printed and as an e-book available at GetSwitchedOn.com. Please let me know what *you think*. Send me an email at Chip@GetSwitchedOn.com with your thoughts about this book and how it impacted you. It is my sincere desire that you find the same pleasure in this book that I have.

Chip Eichelberger

THINK

1.

We all enter the world with an abundance of nerve energy, and by conserving that energy we can adapt and adjust our nerve equipment to keep pace with the progress and evolution of our times.

The way to preserve and conserve nerve equilibrium and power is to rest and relax the nerves each day.

You may rest them by a change of the thought habit each day, by relaxation, by sleep, and by the suggestions made in this book.

There are but few advance danger signals shown by the nervous system, and in this there is a marked difference between the nerves and the organic system.

If you abuse your stomach, head, heart, lungs, liver, kidneys or eyes, you have distress and pain.

The nervous energy is like a barrel of water — you can draw water from the faucet at the bottom until you have almost exhausted the contents.

Nature mends ordinary nerve waste each day, like the rains replenish the cistern.

A reasonable use of your nerve force, like a reasonable use of the rainwater, **Conserve your energy.** means you can maintain a permanent supply. But you must be reasonable; you must give the cistern a chance to refill and replace that which you have drawn out.

You, who have shattered and tattered your nerves, are not hopeless. You can come back, but it must be done by complete change of the acts that brought on the condition.

Get more sleep. Eliminate the useless, harmful fads, fancies and functions which disturbed and prevented you from living a sane, rational life.

Avoid extremes, cultivate rhythm and *regularity* in your business and your home life. Keep away from excitement. Read really good books. Walk more, talk less.

Eat less heat-making foods and more apples. Follow the diet, exercise and thought rules suggested in "Pep."

Maybe these lines are being read by a discouraged one who is "all nerves," which means lost nerve force. To **No Need** you I say there is hope and cheer **To Despair.** and strength and courage if, right here, now, you resolve to cut the actions, habits and stunts that knocked you out and follow my suggestions.

I know, my friend, for I've trotted the heat, danced the measure, and been through the mill.

Now I am fearless, calm and prepared. I can stand any calamity, meet any issue, endure any sorrow.

I can do prodigious work in an emergency, go without rest or eating when required, because I have poise, efficiency peace.

I realize nothing is as bad as it is **Steer A** painted. **Middle** Nothing is as good as its boosters **Course.** claim. I go in the middle of the road, avoiding extremes. I have confidence in my heart. Courage, hope, happiness, and content attend me on my way. I've buried envy in a deep pit and covered it with quick lime.

I am keeping worry out by keeping faith, hope and cheer thoughts in my brain-room, and these are antiseptics against the ravages of the worry microbe.

I have my petty troubles and little make-believe worries, just enough of them to make me realize I *have them* licked, and to remind me I must not let up on my mastery of them.

Worry growls once in a while just to make me grab tighter the handle of my whip.

And you may enjoy this serene state, too. There is no secret about it. I will gladly give you the rules of the game in this book. Just prepare to receive some practical, helpful suggestions.

2.

You are a busy person, so am I. Busy persons are the ones who do things. The architect is a busy man, but he has learned that the effort spent in preparing his plans is the
How to most important part of his work.
Use Your The plans enable him to do his work
Assets. systematically and lay down rules and methods to get the highest efficiency and accomplishment from those who do the work of erecting the building.

If the architect would order lumber, stone and hardware, without system, and start to erect the building without carefully prepared *plans*, the building would lack symmetry and strength, and it would be most expensive.

The planning time therefore was time well spent.

Few persons have the ability to control and *conserve* their talents so as to produce the highest efficiency. Men rush along thinking their busyness means business. Really, it means double energy and extra moves to produce a given *effect*.

The elimination of unnecessary moves means operating along lines of least resistance, and any
plan or method that will help to do
Unnecessary away with unnecessary moves and
Moves. make the necessary moves more potential will be received with welcome, I am sure.

With the object of conserving energy and strengthening your force, this book is written.

It shall not be a book of ultimate definiteness

or a book of exact science. There are no definite or exact rules that will apply, without exception, to any science except mathematics.

But we shall learn many helpful truths, nevertheless, and if I err, or disagree with your conclusions, just eliminate those lines and take the helps you find. I particularly emphasize the importance of taking a few minutes each evening and using the time for sizing up things, by inventory, analy-sis, speculation, comparison and hypothesis. Many of the great captains of industry who are noted for their energy in accomplishing things worth while, have learned the value of this daily habit.

I want to help YOU to form the habit of thinking over each day's activities in the quiet, relaxed, uncolored, unprejudiced, secluded environment of your home.

When the day's work is over, spend fifteen or twenty minutes each evening in seclusion, and with closed eyes, size yourself up. Think over your daily round and the work you **Know** are doing. Are you getting the best **Thyself.** out of yourself? Or are you plodding along aimlessly, scattering your energy in a haphazard, hit-or-miss fashion that benefits nobody? Are you growing, or are you standing still? In these fifteen-minute sizing-up sessions, you will come to grips with yourself. You will see yourself as you really are, and will discover your weaknesses, your strength, your real worth.

I have chosen the evening as the time for our little talks. In the evening we can be cozy, comfy and communicative. The bank is closed. We met the note and got through the day. We are alive and well; we can open our hearts. There is no office boy to disturb us, and the life insurance agent is away at his club.

Yes, we can be alone and tranquilly let down the tension, lower the speed and, with normal heartbeats play the low tones, the soft strains, the quieting music, and soothe our nerves.

All day we've heard the band with its drums and trombones and shrieky music. The day with its busy whirl kept our analyzing mental think-tank occupied with thoughts of gain and game and fame.

In the evening we have time to study logic and to reason, to analyze and to take inventory, to thresh out problems.

So let us relax and reflect in the evening quiet.

3.

Man's nature makes it imperative for him to be interested in something.

That interest is to his help or hurt, according as he directs it.

There is much worry and misery in the world because so many are astatic, like a compass that has lost its lodestone.

Man is definitely the result of the materials the body and the mind feed upon.

Character is the result of a determined purpose to be and to do right — to one's self and to one's fellows.

The man of character focuses his attention on truth, and on fact.

He uses theories with fact, to aid his progress, but he recognizes that theorizing, without fact as a safety ballast, is a useless **Theory And** expenditure. Theories without fact **Fact.** leave man in a rudderless boat; he gets nowhere, he merely drifts.

Theory often helps to get at fact, but the better way is to get at fact by proven experience, of which there is an inexhaustible abundance in the world.

Facts are based on natural laws. The study of natural laws is beneficial. We shall strive in our studies to keep close to fact with just enough speculation to enliven the interest in facts.

Living the artificial life makes for worry, illness and failure.

Living in harmony with the great natural laws is the helpful way to live.

To abide by the law is safety; to violate the law brings punishment.

Every man is better if he follows scientific methods and habits of thought and living.

The loafing or astatic mind will fall into morbid tendencies.

The employed, truth-seeking, idealistic, hopeful mind is never dependent on people or things for its pleasure.

The acquiring of helpful knowledge, the seeking of worth-while truth, are ever profitable employments, paying present and future dividends, and meanwhile those acts positively divert the thought from morbid tendencies.

I shall strive to bring helpful knowledge, good cheer and interesting facts for your present occupation and benefit.

If I succeed in accomplishing my purpose, even in part, my time has been well spent.

Thought Never Stops. We have an unchallenged fact to rest our feet on, a fact that shall follow us through all the pages of this book, and that is: Our thoughts never stop, our brains never sleep. So then, we must consider that thought current, and reckon with it.

The motive power is turned on, and we must grasp the helm if we sail the sea of life successfully, baffling storms and avoiding rocks.

Scientific books are usually dry, uninviting reading; they lack the human interest. They are generally bloodless skeletons.

We shall try to weave science into new patterns and paint interesting pictures, so that science will attract and not repel.

This book is different in its suggestions, in its prescriptions, in its language, but it is universal with all scientific books, in that its aim is helpful truth.

We go by different routes, but our objective point is the same.

We will avoid technical names and symbols, and will speak the common language that the multitude understands.

We shall deal with problems and aspirations that come to us all in this busy workaday world.

We shall try to cut the underbrush in the swamp and blaze a plain trail out on to the big high road.

We shall keep in step to the drum-beats of truth, we will rest and recreate in cool shady places, and then up and on to our purpose with smiles on our faces, courage in our hearts, and song on our lips.

Every moment of our journey will be worth while and positively helpful if we take the trip with conscientious application and continuity of purpose.

Our path is strewn with roses and thorns; we must enjoy the roses and escape the thorns.

We welcome you, the neophyte, who have joined us in our pilgrimage.

4.

Let's be personal; that's a good way to establish a good idea in place of a bad one.

Are YOU pleasant to live with? Keep this personal question before you, even if you are cocksure that you can answer, yes.

Be Pleasant. Maybe there are some little jars, rattles, gratings, you are not aware of. Few of us are honest when looking for our own faults.

There may be some sand in your gearbox. It won't hurt you to keep the personal question alive for a few days, — "Am I pleasant to live with?"

I love the pleasant people whether they are fat, lean, tall, short, red heads, brown heads, homely, handsome, republicans or democrats, business men or artisans.

The complaining, unpleasant grouch is like a bear with a toothache. Miserable himself and spreading misery all around.

A freckle-faced, red-headed, cross-eyed man with a healthy funny bone will spread more cheerfulness and sunshine than a bench full of sad and solemn justices of the supreme court, or a religious conference.

What a different story would be written of Job, if he had only possessed a servant who could dance a double shuffle and whistle "Dixie" while cooking breakfast.

David was a man after my own heart; he brought gladsome songs into the world. He said, "Live the way of pleasantness."

You can pray, sing, play, work, think, rest, hope; you can be well or ill, rich or poor and still be pleasant to live with.

Being pleasant helps you to be strong in body and mind, and it keeps you young a long time.

A Tonic Quality. **Pleasantness** It's good medicine; I know it. My little motto, "**Be** pleasant every morning until ten o'clock, the rest of the day will take care of itself," has brought sun-shine into many homes.

If you frown it will soon get to be a habit —and give you a heavy heart. If you smile your face will be attractive, no matter how unlucky you were in the lottery of beauty.

Be pleasant and you will never feel old. The pleasant disposition is a sure route to happy land and happy homes.

Old Ponce de Leon lost out in searching for thefountain of youth. If he had been pleasant, he would have kept the smiles on his wife's face and there would have been no excuse to leave her to find the mythical fountain.

Hoe cake, bacon and smiles beat lobster, cham-pagne and frowns.

Our land is thrice blessed with its peaceful, happy homes — for "happy homes are the strength of a nation."

Be pleasant in your home. Make the children feel home is the pleasantest place in the world. Every act and example is written in the child's memory tablet. Let your hours with the children be loving, laughing, living hours. Pat them on the head, joke with them, whisper affection, express love to them. Those acts will be remembered in all their years to come, for you are planting everlasting plants that may pass on to a hundred generations and make children happy a thousand years from now.

Cheerfulness Is Its Own Reward. Be pleasant to live with and you will have more pleasant things to live for. There will be kindnesses, kisses, beauty, health, peace, fun, happiness and content coming your way all along the great big road of life you are traveling.

Be pleasant to live with and the people will turn to you as you pass and reflect your cheerfulness like the sunflowers turn to face the sun.

Be pleasant; don't be cross and crabbed because someone else in the household is not pleasant. Do your part; you will likely thereby cure the frown habit on the face of the unfortunate disturber of your peace.

Make yourself right before you criticise your life partner. Answer this question, "Am I pleasant to live with?"

Don't fool yourself in the matter. Get right down to brass tacks with yourself, watch your moves and acts and attitude for ten days carefully before answering the question.

If your answer is no, now is your time to change your attitude and try the pleasant plan, and here is my blessing and good **wishes in such** an event.

5.

There is fun and interest and diversion all around us. All we need is keen observation and we will see much that passes unnoticed to the preoccupied person.

What an interesting thing is the great round world we live in! The people are as interesting as fish in an aquarium.

See the rushing, surging crowd. Man pushes along searching for necessary things to be done; he builds cities, harnesses rivers, **Sitting On** makes ships to sail the seas to the **The Sidelines.** uttermost parts of the earth. Man goes to war, he builds death-dealing devices that destroy in a few minutes a beautiful cathedral which has taken centuries to build.

Man makes the desert blossom like a rose.

Here is the scientist in his laboratory, trying to unite certain elements to produce new substance. Here is the beauty in her silken nest; here the lover; there the musician; yonder the peanut man, and in the office building is the captain of industry — all busy bees deeply absorbed in their respective interests, and intoxicated in the belief that they are important and greatly necessary.

Yet in the broad measure of ages they are mere ripples on the sea of time, faint bubbles on the eternal deep, and grains of sand at the mountain foot.

Great man by his own measure — minute man by the great measure of time. Mammoths to the near-sighted — mites to the far-sighted. Hustle and bustle, crowd and push. They tramp down the weaker brothers in the mad race after the golden shekels, which are only measures of the ability to buy and own material things; symbols of power to make others serve you. These golden shekels which men fret, sweat and fight for, can only buy physical and material things.

Away from the crowd is the little group who have learned a great truth, which is that happiness is not to be bought with gold. This little minority knows that mental **A Great Truth.** pleasures are best, and that mental pleasures cannot be found on the great highway of material conquest.

The puffy, corn-fed millionaire pities the man who is content to live with small means and enjoy what he has to the full extent.

The wise man is he who gets fullness out of life — happiness, respect, content, freedom from worry; who is busy doing useful things busy helping his brother, busy training his children, busy spreading sunshine and love and the close-together feeling in his home circle.

The corn-fed, hardened, senseless, money-mad, dollar-worshipper knows not peace. Smiles seldom linger on his lips. Peace never rests in his bosom, cheer never lights his **Real** face. He is simply a fighting **Happiness.** machine, miserable in solitude, suffering when inactive and sick when resting.

The money-chaser is up and doing, working like a Trojan, because occupation takes his mind off the painful picture of his misspent opportunity and his destroyed natural instinct. When fighting for gold he forgets his appalling poverty in the really worth-while things in the world.

Like the drunkard in his cups, the intoxication makes him forget, and he is negatively happy.

Money received as reward for doing things worth-while is laudable.

We cannot sit idly by and neglect to earn money to provide food, shelter and education for our loved ones, but between times we should seek the wealth that comes from right mental employment.

The millionaire thinks, dreams and gets dollars, and that is all.

The worth-while man thinks kindness, usefulness, self-improvement, brotherhood, love and he gets happiness.

The man who discovers means to help his fellow man, does a good act, but is the man with the dollars in front of his eyes who commercializes the discovery and invention. In the end, the man that helped mankind fares better than the man who made the millions.

Doing For Others.

It's a great crowd surging by, and very few have the good sense to learn the value of TODAY. That great crowd I see below my win-dow thinks ever of tomorrow and forgets the wondrous opportunities that today holds out.

Those who think always of tomorrow will never get the beauties and joys from life that comes to the little group of Today, who appreciates and enjoys the real Now, rather than the pictured Tomorrow that never comes.

It's mighty interesting to sit on the side lines

and watch the crowds go by and speculate on their movements.

Save up your pennies, measure everything by the dollar standard, think **The Road To** dollars, dream dollars, work, **Disillusionment.** slave, push for the dollars and you will build a fortune. You will never have peace or recreation or joy; you will live only in hope of a some day when you will retire. That's the way the millionaires travel life's highway.

Some day the paper will announce the death of those millionaires, and then the dollars will be blown in by reckless heirs, and so the grinding wheels roll on.

Surely there are many ways of looking at things. Surely there is much of interest in the crowd. Surely there is an unending amount of thought and speculation possible about that crowd way down on the street below my window.

What passions, what hopes, what joys, what sorrows, are in the hearts of that hurrying, worrying crowd.

What noise this din of traffic makes; what activity man has stirred up.

A picture, a drama, a tragedy, a comedy — all these I see in the human ants that run along below the hive where I sit and write these lines.

The phone rings and my little Nancy Lou's voice says, " Daddy, will you please bring me a pencil and a tablet with lines on it."

So I must needs stop this, whatever you may call it, and push through the crowd to get that tablet with " lines on it " for my Nancy Lou; and there is some feeling of happiness and content and peace in Daddy's heart as he lays down his pen, for Daddy is going Home, and that word means a lot in his little family, where they all say " Daddy " instead of Papa or Father.

6.

It is hard enough to do duty once, but doubly hard when you anticipate mentally everything you have to do tomorrow. This doing

Wasted Energy. things twice is a habit easily acquired if you don't watch out, and it means wasted energy.

I have just read the experience of a housewife who was resting on a couch and reading. Her eye caught sight of a book lying on the floor across the room.

Instantly her "mindometer", if I may coin a word, registered, "When you get up, pick up that book."

She went on reading, but her mind was not on the magazine she held, but on that book on the floor.

So obsessed did she become that she was miserable until she got up and picked up the book.

I was talking with a woman who was resting on her porch. Her day's work was over. She was dressed for the afternoon. Everything in the home was neat, sweet, clean and tidy. All was serene but her face, and that was the window

Doing Things Twice. through which I saw worry working overtime.

By strategy I learned the trouble, and here is her story: "Tomorrow a lot of fruit will be ready to preserve. I am worrying where I shall put it. My fruit closet is full."

The woman had every reason to say to herself, "Sufficient unto the day," yet she was doing the preserving mentally today and tomorrow she would do the work physically. A tired mind is harder to rest than a tired body, so we must nip this advance mental work in the bud.

We have all been mentally obsessed with worrying about the things we were going to take on our trip; then worrying over the routine of our work when we should return from our trip.

If the housewife looks over her week's work and washes the dishes, makes the beds, cooks the meals, dresses the children, mends the clothes, and does all these things in her imagination before she does them in reality, she is indeed a hard working woman.

It's all right to plan your work; that's economy in mental expenditure, for it simplifies, systematizes, and saves work.

Plan your work in advance, but do not keep your mind on the plans until the work is done. When you have planned, then close the mental book of tomorrow'sduty, and turn to pleasures, rest, relaxation and enjoyment of today.

It is to get a definite, different thought habit fixed that I ask you to give me these few minutes each day, so that we may consider various phases of life, science, pleasure, morals and mental refreshment.

True, we can only have a fleeting look at things, but we'll get enough, I hope, to freshen your minds, change the humdrum, and elicit interest in things. Maybe these heart-to-heart, confidential chats will help us and keep us from going through the mental motions of tomorrow's physical work.

If these evening talks interest you, help clear your vision, help cheer you, help rest you, then they are good for you, and because they help you, they certainly benefit me and make me very happy, because happiness comes from doing something for others.

I write as the mood strikes me, or as a phase of life comes before me, or as an idea strikes in and just won't let go until I grasp my pen and let the words flow.

I mean this book to be human, and not a studied literary effort.

I want to reach you right there alone in the room where you are reading this, and I want the suggestions, the good, the help, to soak in, and I want you to pass the good you get to your brother; you won't lose a bit by doing so.

7.

"She is all right her only trouble is her NERVES." How often we hear that and how little does the person with steady nerves appreci-ate the tortures of " nerves."

A cut, a bruise, a headache, or any of the physical ailments can be quickly cured. Nature will mend the break, but tired, worn, stretched, abused nerves take time to restore. These nerve ailments call for most vigorous mental treatment.

About Nerves.

Neurasthenia means debilitated or prostrated nerves and it shows itself first of all by worry. Worry means the inability to relax the attention from a definite fear or fancied hard luck. Worry leads to many physical and mental disorders.

Left alone this worry stage develops into an acute state and brings with it nervous prostration, and sometimes a complete collapse of the will power.

Before the acute stage of neurasthenia is reached, there is noticed "brain fag," (mental exhaustion) and brain fag is nature's warning signal calling upon you to take notice and change your mental habits.

Worry sometimes develops into hysteria; again it takes the form of hypochondria or chronic blues. The hypochondriac has a chronic, morbid anxiety about personal health and personal welfare. Frequently this state is accompanied by melancholia.

Meloncholia (extreme depression) is the fork in the road. One turning leads to incurable insanity, the other to curable melancholia.

Right here is where heroic action is needed by the sufferer.

Here is where the sufferer must exert his maximum will power, and change completely his

Cure The Worry Habit.

mental and physical habits and his surroundings. Occupation, changed habits, taking in of confidence, faith and courage thoughts — these changes are necessary to the victim of melancholia, or he will shatter his health on the danger rocks and go to pieces.

Melancholia is an ailment that offers a good chance for Christian Science. Mental suggestion, the powerful personality of a friend, and the personal help such a friend can give by counsel, example and suggestion, are all helps.

I have abundant evidence that melancholia sufferers can be restored to peace, efficiency and poise, by proper thought direction, and by proper physical employment.

"Pep," which has principally to do with mental efficiency, definitely lays down rules and practical suggestions for the employment of the mind and body. I have letters and verbal proofs in quantity proving the efficiency of those rules and suggestions.

So wonderful have been the results, so numerous the recoveries, that the testimonials, if published, would make the fake nerve tonic manufacturer die of envy.

"Only your nerves." I cannot understand why

The Importance Of Nerves.

the word, only, is used. It makes it appear that nerves are of minor importance. Nerves are less understood than anything in the human anatomy and they are harder to understand.

Experience has proved that nerves cannot be restored by dope, patent medicines, tonics or prescriptions.

The cure must come by and through the individual possessing the nerves, and by and through the individual's power of will and mastery of the mind.

Get the mental equipment right. Let the mind master the body. Let the nerve sufferer get hold of himself and fill his brain with faith — thought instead of fear — thought, with courage instead of cowardice, with strength instead of weakness, with hope instead of despair, with smiles instead of frowns, with occupation instead of sluggishness, and wonders will appear.

The little shredded, tingling nerve-ends will then commence to synchronize instead of fight, to harmonize instead of breaking into discord, to build instead of destroy.

The building, or coming back to a normal state, is slow; it takes time, patience and will power, but it can be done. I know. I have been through the mill, and I **You Can** pass the word to you and try to stir **"Come Back."** you to be up and doing, even as I did.

Your nerves can be steadied, your thoughts uplifted, your health restored, your ambition re-established, your normality fixed.

Smiles, love and content are to be yours. Poise, efficiency, peace, your blessings. Health, happiness and hope your dividends. All these I promise you if you will read this book from cover to cover, think, and follow its plain, practical teachings.

The curriculum is not hard; it is not my discovery. I am merely the purveyor of facts, the gleaner of truth, and the selector of helpful experiences, first of all for my own benefit, and having proved the truth in my own case, for friends to whom I pass the truths and rules.

I made bold to write books, but the writing has paid me well, not alone in dollars, but from having done a helpful thing in writing for other humans who have had problems, worries and nerves.

The big books on nerves are discouraging and forbidding by their immensity and the labyrinth of technical, scientific terms. There are fine for teachers, but discouraging for the layman.

The great everyday crowd is the class I want to talk to, and so I endeavor to write in plain human, sincere style from heart to heart, with understanding, feeling, charity and sympathy.

I have felt the things you feel, and if I can by example, emphasis, suggestion, rule or good intent, be a help to you, then I have done a service.

8.

There are men who cannot be kept down by circumstances or obstacles.

These men "carry on" with confidence in their hearts and smiles on their faces. They do not lie in wait for the band wagon or favorable winds; they make things happen. They are alert and alive to every favorable opportunity and helpful influence that comes their way.

The Men Who Do Things.

These men are men of good health. They are out of doors much; they carry their heads high and breathe in good air deeply. They greet friends with a smile and put meaning and feeling into every hand clasp.

Let's you and I follow their trail, for it leads out on to the big road.

Do not fear being misunderstood; right will finally come into its own.

We will keep our minds off our enemies, and keep our thoughts on our purpose; we will make up our minds what we want to do. We will mark a straight line on the log and hew to that line.

Fear is the dope drug that kills initiative; hate the poison that shatters clear thinking.

Hate and fear are the iron ore in our life's vessel; they deflect the compass and prevent us from holding to the course.

There are splendid worth-while things for us to do, and with continuity of action and singleness of purpose on our part the days will pass by as we are seizing opportunity and making

Grasp Present Opportunities.

use of the things required for the fulfillment of our desires. We are like the coral insect that takes from the running tide the material to build a solid fortress. Our running tide is made up of the gliding golden days.

Let's waste no time in trying to make friends or in seeking to attach ourselves to others. True friends are not caught by pursuit; they come to us; they happen through circumstances we do not create.

Self-reliance is ours, and we must first use it for our own betterment. We will then have a surplus of energy to allow us to help others.

Our energy hours must be devoted to our purposes and ideals. Atween times, we must rest and relax, and repair the waste that strenuosity (intense energy) makes.

Breathe good air, bask in the sunshine, see nature, and say to yourself: "All these treasures are for me; all these things I am part of."

The Joy Of Living. Do not prepare for death; prepare for life. Preparing for death brings the end before your allotted time. Like Job of old, that which we fear will come to us.

We must not think of death, or waste time preparing for it. It makes us miserable today. It makes us weak and fills us with fear, and it draws the day of our departure nearer.

Today is ours. Live freely, fully today. Be unafraid, unhurried, and undisturbed.

We are building character, and the way we build it is by mental attitude, by our acts, and by the way we employ the precious moments of today.

THINK

Put yourself in harmony with nature realize the wonderful power of the will —and you will be strong, a veritable king among men.

9.

The calamity howler is found everywhere. in times of peace or war he is with us. This pessimist sows seeds of discord, plants envy,

The Pessimist. generates the anarchist spirit, and is an all around nuisance.

A man may spend years erecting a building; a fiend can demolish it in a minute with a stick of dynamite.

The calamity howler is a destroyer; he doesn't think, he spurts out words. His words and arguments are simply parrot mimicry and void of intellectual impulse, as are the movements of an angle worm.

These gloom merchants talk of their rights, and they expect and demand the same privileges and benefits that are earned by the man who uses his head.

The pessimist sees good in nobody. Human nature to him is a cesspool of villainy and corruption. He will not tolerate a word of praise for a thing well done. Disparagement is his favorite weapon. He ascribes mean and selfish motives to public-spirited men. Every deed of kindness, every act of generosity, is given a sinister meaning when seen in the light of his own base soul.

At home he is a grumbler and a grouch. His presence depresses, and happiness fades away at his approach.

In the community, he never reaches high office because he lacks civic spirit and the forward looking view. He obstructs progress instead of promoting it.

At his work, he lags behind where others achieve. He rails at conditions instead of changing them, and eventually he finds himself shelf ed and shunned as a back number.

These purveyors of panic eat into the vitals of the nation. They breed discontent, undermine morale, and sow suspicion and distrust where previously there had been friendliness, cooperation and the pull-together spirit.

Wherever men gather, you will find these ghoulish spirits. They are in evidence in times of peace and plenty, as well as in times of war and peril.

It matters not that our farmers are seeing to it that our granaries are filled today as never before, and that every man has a job. These prophets of disaster have only one string to their harp, and they will twang on that and no other.

The Danger of Pessimism. In times of war, the pessimist is doubly dangerous, for he spreads his iniquitous propaganda among people who are already under a great emotional strain.

Always a menace, when a people are in the throes of a great life-and-death struggle, it is doubly necessary to stamp out this destroyer of morale, with his insidious campaign of gloom and despair and his veiled innuendos of panic and destruction.

It is up to you and to me to denounce these breeders of discord; to hold them up to the scorn of intelligent, thinking people. They are neither doers nor thinkers, and the world has no need of them in these trying times.

10.

This evening I rode home in a crowded street car. What an interesting study it was to watch the faces in that car.

Discontent, discomfort, worry, gloominess on nearly every face. Tired faces, tired bodies drooped over from a hard day's work, mouth corners depressed. Hopelessness stamped on the countenances.

As the people came in the car, some of them had smiles or at least passable expressions, but **Gloom and Cheer.** when they got crowded together and saw the gloomy faces, the gloom spread to their faces, too. At a picnic, all are smiling and laughing.

In the street car at six o'clock, the long procession of workers is a stream of solemn faces. Contagion, example, surroundings, yes, that's it — contagion and example.

At six o'clock in the cars, all is gloom, blueness and sorrow faces. At eight o'clock many of these faces will be changed; there will be joy, smiles, **Good Cheer Contagious.** rosiness, singing and dancing. Yet the actual conditions of finance, health, hope or prospects haven't changed since these people were in the car at six o'clock.

Why, then, such a change in two hours?

It is this: At seven o'clock these workers sat down to supper; they were out of that gloom-reflected street car atmosphere.

Now they are talking; they are rounding-up the day's activities; they are HOME with mother, sister, brother and the kiddies. The home ones greet them with smiles, the appetizing supper pleases the palate, good cheer permeates, and all around them is smiles and joy.

Gloom spreads gloom. Joy spreads joy. Gloom is black; joy is white. One darkens, the other brightens.

Well, then, where's the moral? What's the benefit from this little study of the street car passengers?

The lesson is plain: It is that you and I are ferments of joy, or acids of gloom. We are influences to help or to hurt. To hurt others by our example hurts us. To help others by our example helps us. We become happier than ever.

In the street car, life was not worth living if you judged by the pained faces. In two hours, by changed thought, the example of life was worth while.

What changes mental attitude makes!

"When a man has spent His very last cent,
The world looks blue, you bet;
But give him a dollar, And loud he will holler
There's life in the old world yet."

Next time we get on the street car, let's plant some smiles. Let's give that lady a seat and smile when we do it.

We can spread cheer by merely wearing a cheery face. Costs little, pays big. Let's do it.

11.

Some of our richest blessings are gained by not striving for them directly. This is so true that we accept the blessings without thinking about how we came to get them.

Particularly true is this in the matter of happiness. Everyone wants to be happy, but few know how to secure this blessing. **Be Happy.** Most people have the idea that the possession of material things is necessary to happiness, and that idea is what keeps architects, automobile makers, jewelers, tailors, hotels, railroads, steamships and golf courses busy.

Do your duty well, have a worth-while ambition, be a dreamer, have an ideal, keep your duty in mind, be occupied sincerely with your work, keep on the road to your ideal, and happiness will cross your path all the while.

Happiness is an elusive prize; it's wary, timid, alert and cannot be caught. Chase it and it escapes your grasp.

I read today of a friend who walked home with a workman. This is the workman's story: He had a **One Man's Story.** son who was making a record in school. He had two daughters who helped their mother; he had a cottage, a little yard, a few flowers, a garden. He worked hard in a garage by day, and in the evening he cultivated his flowers, his garden, and his family. He had health, plus contentment a-plenty. His possessions were few and the care of them consequently a negligible effort.

Happiness flowed in the cracks of his door. Smiles were on his lips, joy in his heart, love in his bosom; that's the story my friend heard.

Then came a friend in an automobile on his way home from the club. He picked up my friend, and unfolded to him a tale of woe, misery and discontent.

This club man had money, automobiles, social standing, possessions, and all the objects and material things envious persons covet—yet he was unhappy. His whole life was spent chasing hap-piness, but his sixty horsepower auto wasn't fast enough to catch it.

The poor man I have told you about was the man who washed the club man's auto.

The strenuous pleasure seeker fails to get happiness; that is an inexorable law. He developsinto a pessimist with an acrid, satirical disgust at all the simple, wholesome, worth-while, real things in life.

This is not a new discovery of mine; it's an old truth. Read Ecclesiastes, the pessimistic chronicle of the Bible, and you'll learn what comes to the pleasure-chaser, and you will know about "vanity and vexation of spirit."

Do something for somebody. Engage in moves and enterprises that will be of **Making Others** service to the community and **Happy.** help the uplift of mankind. This making others happy is a positive insurance and guarantee of your own happiness.

You must keep a stiff upper lip, a stiff backbone; you must forget the wishbone and the envious heart.

Paul had trials, setbacks, hardships and hard labors; he had defeats and discouragements and still the record shows he was "always rejoicing."

Paul was a man of Pep. In the dungeon, with his feet in stocks, he sang songs and rejoiced. Paul was happy, ever and always, not because he strove to get happiness, but because he had dedicated his life to the service of mankind.

The real hero, the real man of fame, the real man of popularity, doesn't arrive by setting out on a quest for any of these things; the result is incidental.

The real hero forgets self first of all; that is the essential step to greatness.

Washington at Valley Forge had no thought that his acts there would furnish inspiration for a picture that would endure for generations.

Lincoln, the care-worn, tired, noble man, in his speech at Gettysburg, never dreamed that that speech would stamp him as a master of words and thought, in the hearts of his country-men. He thought not of self. He was trying to soothe wounds, cheer troubled spirits, and give courage to those who had been so long in shadow-land.

Ever has it been that fame, glory, happiness came as rewards, not to those who strive to capture, but to those who strive to free others from their troubles, burdens and problems.

12.

I am often asked: "Are you happy ALL the time?" My answer is no.

A continuous state of happiness cannot be enjoyed by any human. There are no pans, no

Continuous Happiness Impossible. habits, no methods of living that will insure unbroken happiness.

Happiness means periods or marking posts in our journey along life's road. These high points of bliss are enjoyed because we have to walk through the low places between times.

Continuous sunshine, continuous warm weather, continuous rest, continuous travel, continuous anything spells monotony. We must have variety.

We need the night to make us enjoy the day, winter to make us enjoy summer, clouds to make us enjoy sunshine, sorrow to make us enjoy happiness.

But, dear reader, mark this: We can be philosophical, and have content, serenity and poise between the happiness periods.

When you get blue, or have dread or sorrow, or possess that indescribable something that makes you feel badly; when you have worry or trouble, then's the time to get hold of your thinking machinery and dispel the shadows that cross your path.

Occupation and focusing your thoughts on your blessings these are the methods to employ.

As long as you dwell upon your imagined or your real sorrows, you will be miserable and the worries will magnify like gathering clouds in April.

Change your thoughts to confidence, faith, and good cheer, and busy your hands with work.

Think of the happiness periods you have had and know that there are further happiness dividends coming to you. Keep this sort of thought, and with it, useful occupation, and the sunshine will dispel your gloomy forebodings and sorrow thoughts like the sun dispels the April showers, bringing about a more beautiful day because of the clouds and storms just passed.

Think Happiness.

When trouble or sorrows come, sweeten your cup with sugar remembrances of joys that have been and joys you are to have.

Envy no one; envy breeds worry. The person you would envy has his sorrows and shadows, too. You see him only when the sunlight is on the face; you don't see him when he is in shadow-land.

No, dear ones, I, nor you, nor anyone on earth can have complete, unruffled, continued happiness, but we can brace up and call our reserve will-power, reason, and self-confidence into action when we come to the marshy places along the road. We can pick our steps and get through the mire, and sooner than we believe it possible, we can get on the good solid ground; and as we travel, happiness will often come as a reward for our poise and patience.

My friends say: " You always seem happy," and in that saying they tell a truth, for I am happy often — very, very often — and between times I make myself seem to be happy. This making myself "seem to be happy " gives me serenity, contentment, fortitude, and the very " seeming " soon blossoms into a reality of the condition I seem to be in.

You can be happy often, and when you are not happy, just seem to be happy anyway; it will help you much.

13.

A little child is crying over a real or fancied injury to her body or to her pride.

So long as she keeps her mind on the subject she is miserable.

Distract her attention, get her mind on another subject, and her tears stop and smiles replace frowns.

This shows how we are creatures of our thoughts. "As a man thinketh in his heart, so is he" is a truth that has endured through the centuries.

We are children in so far as we cry and suffer when we think of our ills or hurts or wrongs or bad luck.

We can smile and have peace, poise and strength if we change our thoughts to faith, courage and confidence.

Fear-Thought And Faith-Thought. Our condition is what we make it. If we think fear, worry and misery, we will suffer. If we think faith, peace and happiness, we will enjoy life. Every thought that comes out of our brain had to go in first. The kind of thoughts we have afford an indication of the kind of people we are.

If we feed our brain storehouse with trash and fear and nonsense, we have poor material to draw from.

The last thought we put in the brain before going to sleep is most likely to last longest. Soit is our duty to quietly relax, slow down, to eliminate tear-thought and self-accusation, and to

Thought Control. substitute some good helpful thought in closing the mental book of each day.

Therefore read a chapter or two from a worth-while book the last thing before going to bed.

Say to yourself, " I am unafraid; I can, I will awake in the morning with smiles on my face, courage in my heart, and song on my lips."

These suggestions for closing the day will be of instant help to you.

The great power for good the wherewith to give you strength, progress and efficiency — is within yourself and at the command of your will.

You can't think faith and fear, good and bad, courage and defeat, all at the same time.

You can only think one thing at a time.

Your great power is your will, and the wherewith to help yourself is your thought habit.

Change your thought habit as you go to bed. You can do it; it's a matter of will determination. The more faithful you are to your purpose, the easier your task will be. Be patient, conscientious, rational and confident.

You are what your thoughts picture you to be. Your will directs your thoughts.

Don't get discouraged if you can't suddenly change your life from shadow to sunshine, from illness to wellness.

Big things take time and patience. The great ship lies in the harbor pointed North. A tug boat could make a sudden pull and break the great chain or tow line.

Yet you could take a half-inch rope and with your own hands turn the great ship completely around by pulling steadily and patiently. The movement would be slow, but it would be sure and you would finally accomplish your purpose.

Don't jerk and fret and be impatient with yourself. You have been for years perhaps worrying and thinking fear-thoughts. You have put a lot of useless and harmful material in your brain.

You can't clean all your brain house in a day or a week, but you can do a little cleaning each day.

You can take the faith-rope of good purpose and start to pull gently, and finally you will turn your whole life's character toward the port of success.

The great crowd worries; only the few have learned the power of the will, and the benefits to be derived from mental control.

Business and social duties call for strong men and woman. You can't reach mastership if you remain a siave.

Your first duty is to yourself, and success or failure is your reward exactly in proportion as you exercise your will power and handle your thought habits.

14.

The doctors are giving less medicine and doing more in the way of suggesting diet and exercise rules, sanitation and preventive practices.

The Best Medicine. Medicine is mostly poison and its effect is to shock the organs or glands to bring about reaction. Nature makes the cure.

In emergency drugs are all right, but the doctor and not the individual should settle the matter of what drug to use and the proper time to use it.

When there's a pain or disease, it's due to congestion of some organ, to infection, or to improper nourishment, or improper habits.

Ninety percent of aches, pains and ailments can be cured by a dominant mental attitude and by proper attention to eating and exercise.

The habitual medicine user is not cured by the medicine but by nature; the medicine simply serves as a means to establish mental control and to create confidence in the sufferer that he is to get well.

Recently I spent much time in a large hospital visiting a relative who had been operated on. I know several members of the staff of doctors and nurses.

I have seen many operations, some very heroic ones, and my appreciation of the good work of good surgeons is greatly augmented by the wonderful helps I have seen them bring to suffering humanity.

I have talked with scores of patients and

watched the progress of their cases.

I have b plausible logic, mental suggestion, and good Cheer to the hospital patients, brought many a smile through a mist of tears.

I have seen the wonderful results of mental suggestion to the discouraged patients.

To show the effects that faith-thought will produce, I will relate some instances.

Mental Sickness. One patient screaming for a hypodermic injection to relieve her pain was given an injectionof sterilized water and the pain vanished. Another just could not sleep without her bromide (sedative). The nurse fixed up a powder of sugar, salt and flour; the patient took the powder and went to sleep. That was mind control and mental longing satisfied.

Another patient had to take something to stop her pains; she got capsules of magnesia. The capsule satisfied her longing, established her faith and gave her relief; the relief was through her mind and not through the capsule.

I have seen several weary, despondent patientsfretting and wearing themselves out over

Changing Thought Direction. their so-called weakness and run-down condition. I 1-12,²-: placed copies of "Pep" in their -Is and watched courage, faith, cheer and serenity .orcie to them. It diverted their minds from self-doubt and self-accusation to faith-thought, confidence and courage.

You can think of only one thing at a time, and "Pep" or any other book that can change the thought habit from fear to faith, from worry to peace, is doing a service.

I've been in shadowland in the hospital to see

for myself the actual help that mental control will bring to sufferers, and the evidence is far above my powers to describe.

I've seen the patient's eyes brighten up when the cheery surgeon came with hope, smiles and confidence on his face.

I've seen the drooping of spirits when well-meaning but poor-expressing friends came into the patient's room and condoned and sorrowed with him.

Verily, "as a man thinketh in his heart, so is he."

Verily, good cheer and good thought are good medicines.

And to these truths all good doctors say "Amen! "

15.

How often we see the pill fiend. In his vest pocket he has a small apothecary shop — a collection of round paste-board boxes and little bottles. Every little while he dopes

The Pill Fiend. himself. If his stomach is on a strike, he pops in a pill. if his head aches, he takes a tablet. H he sneezes, he takes a cold-cure pill.

When anyone around speaks of a pain or ache, he hands the person a pill.

The pill eater is a hypochondriac, and very likely his doctor knows it. His salvation is that the doctor probably gives him harmless stuff in pill form. The patient doesn't know this, and it's like a rabbit's foot or a piece of pork rubbed on a wart — it satisfies the mind and nature makes the cure.

Often, however, the pills are not innocent; the pill fiend buys the tablets and pills direct from the druggist. The headache tablet is most likely one of the coal tar drugs like acetanilide (pain killer), and that is positively harmful when taken too often.

There are times to take pills in cases of emergency, when you can shock nature with a poison and bring a wholesome reaction.

These times are rare, and the doctor should be the sole judge as to when such treatment is necessary.

Exercise, diet, correct habits of living will prevent the congestion and clogging-up that causes illness and pain.

The pill habit is nothing less than a drug habit, and the drug habit positively **A Dangerous** weakens the system. The headache **Habit.** tablet does not cure the headache; it only stops the pain; the evil is still there. The headache is merely nature's signal that something is out of whack.

Headaches are generally caused by stomach disorders, eye strain, or neuralgia; the latter in turn is caused by too much uric acid in the system.

Eat fruit, drink plenty of water, and that will flush the system and stop stomachic headache.

See the optician if it's eyes. If you have a frequent headache in the forehead, very likely it's the eyes, even though you do not suspect it.

If it's neuralgia, get a corrective diet from the doctor.

I know scores of men, and women, too, who take pills enough to kill a person. Their systems have been educated up to it; they are saturated with poison.

And the worst of it is they never get well while taking the pills; it is only a temporary deadening of the pain.

Then, there are many who take pills to make them sleep. That's a crime. It's self-murder by slow degrees, for they are surely shortening their lives by this poison dope pill habit.

Mark this: Nature, and Nature **Nature the** alone, effects cures, and it's in very, **Curer.** very few instances that a poison pill can be used to advantage.

You can keep well by getting good air, good water, good sunshine, good food, good exercise, good rest, good cheer and good thought. That is what I call my golden prescription, and it will do wonders for you, and every doctor will tell you so.

Pills kill, if you keep up the habit. There are no two ways about it. I say positively and knowingly that this pill habit is absolutely life shortening.

Don't try to argue; the evidence is unshakable on this point.

If you could have seen the derelicts in the hospitals that I have, if you could have seen the wretched bodies, destroyed nerve systems, the broken-down, emaciated, hopeless shells of men and women addicted to the baneful pill habit, you would be as positive as I am that pills kill if you keep up the habit.

Life is sweet and precious to us all. Do not shorten it by taking pills and tablets for every ache or pain. Try nature's way. Realize that mental suggestion and will-power will drive away most pains or temporary aches.

Brace up, cheer up; chuck the pills in the garbage can.

16.

There are two principal kinds of pleasures that man seeks; one is material pleasures, and about ninety-nine per cent of the human family devote themselves to these.

Two Kinds of Pleasure. The remainder the one per cent — seek mental pleasures, and this little group is the one that gets the real, lasting, satisfying and improving pleasures out of life.

The material pleasures are the social pleasures of eating, displaying, possessing, and so forth. Material pleasures generate in the human the desire for fluff, feathers, and four-flushing.

Material pleasures accentuate the desire to possess things, and in the strife for possession, hearts are broken, fortunes wasted, nerves shattered, and the finer sentiments calloused.

The homes where material pleasures abound are the ones where worry, neurasthenia and nervous prostration abound.

Material pleasures are merely stimulants for the time being, and there always come the intermittent reflexes of gloom and depression.

The desire to show off, to excite envy in others, is always present at the homes where material pleasures are the rule.

Material pleasures call for crowds. Mental pleasures are best enjoyed in solitude.

The material pleasure-seeker lives a life of convention, engagements, routine, strain, and high tension.

The person who is so fortunate as to

appreciate and follow mental pleasures is serene, natural, happy and content. A cozy room, loved ones around, music, books, love and social **Mental Pleasures Are Best.** conversation — those are mental pleasures; those are best. He who can pick up a book and read things worth while, gets satisfaction unknown to those whose life is a round of banquets, theaters, dances, automobiles, parties, bridge, clubs and society doings.

When you spend the evening playing cards, the chances are you come home late, and when you retire, it takes perhaps an hour or so before you fall to sleep.

And during the night you dream of cards, of certain hands, of certain circumstances, or certain persons who were prominent in the evening's game.

The reason you do not go to sleep after an exciting evening is that you have set your nerve carburetor at high tension and have forgotten to lower it before you go to sleep.

On the other hand, when you have been reading a restful book, full of good **Good Reading.** thought, you establish an equilibrium, a relaxed state of nerves, and particularly, you have switched the current or direction of your day's thoughts. That change spells rest, and you retire and go to sleep easily.

You will scarcely believe what a wondrous change for the better you will notice in yourself if you make it a rule to have a brain clearing, mental inventory, and nerve relaxation every night before you go to sleep.

Your brain works at night always; oft-times you

have no remembrance of your dreams, but if your last hour, before retiring, was an hour of excitement, tension or unusual occupation, you will likely go over it all again in your dreams.

If you will let nothing prevent your evening period of soliloquy, you will establish your mental habits into a rhythm that will give you peace, rest and benefit.

In the olden days, when most families had evening worship or family prayers, the members of those households slept soundly and restfully.

Particularly was this so because of the habit formed of getting the mind on peaceful, helpful, comforting, soul-satisfying thoughts that remained fresh on the brain tablets as the members of the home circle went to sleep.

Too often the books read in the home circle are all of the exciting, fascinating, highly colored imaginative type. People read stories of love, adventure or crime, and they dream these same things almost every night.

I have found that it pays to read two classes of literature in the same evening. First read your novel, story, or fascinating book, but fif-teen minutes before you are ready to go to sleep, read some good, wholesome, helpful, uplifting book, and that good stuff will be lastingly filed away in your brain.

What to Read. Finish your evening with books that are interesting, yet educational. Such books as "Life of the Bee" by Maeterlinck, or any one of Fabre's wonderful books on insect life; "Riddle of the Universe" by Haeckel; Darwin's books; Drum-mond's "Ascent of Man;" "Walks and Talks in Geological Fields" is a splendid mental night cap; " Power of Silence;" "Physiology of Faith and Fear; "Emerson's "Essays;" Holmes' "Autocrat of the Breakfast Table;" "Rubaiyat" of Omar Khayyam; Tom Moore's Poems; "Plutarch's lives;" Seneca ; Addison; Bulwer Lytton; Hugo; Carlyle's "Sartor Resartus." This latter book will not fascinate you like Carlyle's "French Revolution," but you will learn to love its fine language, its fine analysis of character, of times, and of things.

There are countless books of the good improving kind. Always save one of them for your **What You Gain.** solid reading, after you have read light literature or novels. If you will get the habit, you will notice great benefits and rapid advancement in your mental equipment. You will sleep better, think clearer; you will learn to enjoy mental pleasures more than material pleasures.

Fifteen minutes, then, to be yours, yours alone, in which you quiet, soothe, strengthen and pacify yourself and add abundant resources and assets.

Let the last reading in the evening be something worth storing up in that precious brain of yours, and the good, worth-while deposit will grow and produce beautiful worth-while mental fruit.

Get the home reading habit. Don't overdo it. Call on friends; go to a good picture show once a while, to good concerts, to good Plays, but do not **Don't Overdo It.** make this going-out-in-the-evening-plan a habit. Let it bp merely a dessert, or a rarity. Like candy and ice cream, it is proper and enjoyable when it is not overdone.

The lover of books and home can enjoy the play, because he only goes to plays worth while, and he doesn't overdo it.

The confirmed theater-goer is a pessimist; he roasts nearly every play, and he is universally bored.

When you get started reading worth-while books on science, on history, on geography, on travel, on natural history, you tap an inexhaustible field of pleasure and satisfaction.

At any time, you can pick up your book and be happy.

Waits in railway stations will be opportunities; trips on trains will be pleasant; evenings alone will be enjoyable, if you can get into a book you like.

Mental pleasures are best.

Material pleasures are merely passing shadows — to be enjoyed for the brief moment before they disappear.

17.

The malady "Verbomania" is spreading rapidly. What's that? You have never heard of Verbomania? Well, then, it's taken from verbosus, the Latin word meaning "abounding in words," the using of more words **Verbomania.** than is necessary. Mania, also Latin, means "to rage"— excessive or unreasonable desire. Therefore, Verbomania is the excessive desire to use more words than are necessary.

There is too much talk nowadays and too little thinking. Some persons start their gab carburetors, and they talk and talk mechanically, without any effort spent in thinking. Just like walking, the motion just goes by itself.

Scientists have suggested that perhaps too much talking without thinking is a disease. I don't see that there is any perhaps about it. Dis-ease is an unnatural condition — a function of the mind or body out of its natural order of working.

We know we can sit down and run ideas through our brain without words, and we can use a lot of words without ideas.

You have read whole pages in a book without receiving an idea. One can rattle off words and not have ideas. When the fountain of words flows in a desert of ideas, it's Verbomania.

People in all walks of life have the disease; they talk together too much without any reason other **Think More,** than to take up time or make **Talk Less.** themselves at ease. Pink teas, receptions and society functions are great rookeries for these Verbomania birds to gather and indulge in their gabfest.

The pianist through long practice is able to play a difficult composition without thinking about it; it's automatic; it's habit in action.

The society dodo bird is just as dexterous in spinning words without thought, as the pianist with his difficult piece.

Our rapid mode of living, our conventions and customs are responsible for much of the Verbomania.

I should like to take my Dictophone (tape recorder) to a fussy "afternoon" and record the word evacuations, the footless conversation, the forced pleasantries, the set sentences that mingle into a hum and buzz. A wilderness of words in a barrenness of ideas.

This abuse of the use of speech makes headaches, weariness, worry, unrest; it saps strength, lowers pep, and lessens resistance.

The cure for Verbomania is to keep away from these butterfly buzz bees; put the clothes-pin of caution on your lips; spend more time alone with your thoughts. Nourish your idea plants that have been starved; prune your word plants.

Don't expose yourself to the crowds where the Verbomaniacs gather. The disease is contagious; it's easy to acquire and hard to retire.

These are ideas put in type to convey a truth for the benefit of all who read these lines, and it is some truth, too.

18.

Love builds homes, gold builds houses. The home has a mongrel dog which is called Prince, and all the family love it. The house had a pedigreed bull pup that is kept in the barn.

There is all the difference between the family which has a home and the family which has a house. In houses we find broken hearts, worry, nervous prostration, because there **House And** is idleness, artificial-ity and **Home.** aimlessness. In homes we find warm hearts, happiness and love, because those in the home have natural, helpful occupation.

In the house is cold reserve; the occupants read when compelled to stay indoors; they grow crabbed and cross and get into a state of habitual dumbness and selfishness.

In the home there is unselfishness, thoughtfulness, and love expressed. Meal time is joy time; it's the get-together period of smiling faces.

In the house the breakfast table is merely a lunch station in the hurried trip from the bedroom to the office.

The sensitive wife of the house gets stinging remarks that abide with her after the lord and master of the house has departed.

In the home the family gets up **What Makes** plenty early enough. Songs and **A Home.** jokes, kisses and love pats are found; the family is on time, and there is happiness all around.

Homes are sweet, because love is present

Houses built by gold are just hotels.

I've noticed the difference when a friend invites me to come to his home or to his house; the word he uses, home or house, indicates to me what I will find when I go there.

In the house I meet a maid or butler at the door. I see conventional furniture, conventional rooms. I am shown into a conventional waiting room, and I wait conventionally for the hostess to come forward with a stiff backbone, a forced smile, and a languid handshake.

When I go to a home built with love, I find a tidy dressed wife at the door, rosy children, and I get a warm, old-fashioned hand clasp, and a beaming, smiling face that spells welcome.

And the dinner — that, too, tells the difference between the "depend-on-the-cook" establishment and the "wife-who-is-the-boss" home.

At the house is formality and frigidity; at the home is ease and enjoyment. The children of the home make breaks and we love them for it; it's natural instinct and frankness.

In the house is worry; in the home is happiness.

Verily, there's a difference in the atmosphere of the house built with gold and the home built with love; one is worthless existence, the other worth-while living.

19.

I haven't space in this book to give reasons or show proofs for everything I suggest, but I want right here to give you a few definite, short,

Seven Simple Health Suggestions. positive, helpful rules about food, thought, habit and exercise that will pay you the most wonderful dividends in health and happiness.

First—Drink two or three glasses of warm, not hot, water, the first thing when you arise in the morning.

Second—Repeat this resolve as you are drinking the water: "I will be pleasant this morning until ten o'clock, and the rest of the day will take care of itself."

Third—Walk to your office or place of business, unless it is over four miles, in which case walk the first three miles and ride the remainder of the distance.

Fourth—Eat one or two apples every day, and do not insult Nature's proper adjustment by peeling the apple. You want the skin because it has things in it you need for your body, and especially for your brain, and you have especial need of the roughage the skin gives.

Fifth—Spend eight or nine hours a day in bed. I belong to the sixty-three hour club; that means nine hours a day rest, seven days in a week,

Get Enough Sleep. which is sixty-three hours. If, through business, travel or other circumstances, I stay up late one or two nights a week, I balance books before the week is up by taking a rest on Sunday afternoon or going to bed earlier one or two nights.

Sixth—Don't stay in bed Sunday morning. It will make you tired, loggy (lazy), stupid and cross. Get up Sunday, say, a half hour or an hour later than week days. Later in the day take a nap if you wish.

Seventh—Spend fifteen minutes just before going to bed in quiet, relaxed solitude. This is the time to slow down your tension, relax your muscles and soothe your nerves.

These rules you can easily remember and if you follow them as I hope you will, the red blood will course in your veins and joy will be in your countenance and the halo of happiness will be around your face.

20.

Every once in a while the human has a negative day. Every act, thought, or spoken sentence has a but, a don't, a can't, or some other negative attachment to it.

The children laugh, play and cut up in the morning, and mother says: "I don't know what I shall do with you, you are just **The Negative** wearing me out. This puts a fear-**Attitude.** thought and a weakness-germ both in mother and the kiddies.

On Sunday afternoon the family is resting. Mother maybe gets the blues, and says: "What's the use, I never get anywhere, go any place; it's just grind, work and worry all the time."

Mother worries because there's a leak in the roof and the water stained the paper in the spare room. She worries because she lives in a rented house, and says: "I have no heart to fix things up because this is a rented house."

This negative thought brings, on a misery state; it's worry, and the worry comes because you dwell on the off side of things. You rehearse your problem, you go over your work, you count your obstacles, and you pile up the negative and fear thoughts.

Bless you, my dear sister, I know what this negative can't, don't, but, and what's-the-use **Next Time,** thought is and how it brings **Show Your** misery. I know how the children **Positive Side.** get on your nerves and make you say "don't" all day to them.

There's only one way to drive out this negative

thought and that is to switch your will power to the positive current. You have a negative day and the fear-thoughts come, just start in one by one and count your blessings of health, blessings of home, and blessings of love.

Nothing can hurt you. You've been through these negative days time and time again; the clouds gathered, you were blue, lonesome, homesick and heartsick, but next day you got busy with work, and occupation drove away the clouds, and the sunshine came. The next Sunday you get in this negative state, just put on your hat and go out to see some neighbor, or go to the park, or take a walk.

Don't sit and stew and fret over your magnified troubles.

Let the children play and laugh; they are not hurting anyone. God bless them. They don't have worries; their little lives are all too short. Their example of smiles and laughter should make you happy. Soon, too soon, they will grow up and go their ways in life and how precious will be the memories of their carefree, golden, happy childhood days.

Cut out envy; that's a mighty bad negative wire. It's the devil's favorite food to make worry and discontent.

Many of the people you envied in the past are dead and buried. Many of the **Envy Makes Worry.** people you envy now are at heart miserable, and you wouldn't envy them if you could look through the artificial outside and know their real hidden thoughts and lives.

"What's-the-use" — that's a bad thing to say; it

plants worry seed.

You are all right; you have far more blessings than sorrows. You can never be entirely free from troubles, care or little irritations.

Rise superior to these things; those around you are affected by and susceptible to your influence and example.

If you have a "but," an "if " or a "don't" tied to every command to your children, they will recognize your uncertainty and your negative, hurtful attitude, and they will take your threats, as well as your promises, with a grain of salt.

Be careful in giving commands; don't put a Spanish bit in the children's mouths to jerk them and torture them.

Be positive, make your promises and orders stick, and the kiddies will soon know you mean what you say.

Exposing Your Weakness. These negative "driving me crazy" attachments to your commands spell weakness, and make you drive, cajole and spin out your orders, and the children hesitate and are slow to obey. Let them see your positive side. Let them learn to obey with a "yes, mamma" spirit, and your orders will be less frequent, shorter, and they will be obeyed on the instant.

The kiddies learn to size you up, mamma, and if they see a wobbly, worried, despondent, unsure attitude in you, they will discount your threats and make allowances, saying: "That's mamma's way."

Don't show your cry side but show your smile side.

Sunday is a great trial day for you, mamma, but don't let your negative wires get the best of you.

THINK

Sing as you make the beds and tidy up; let sunshine in and drive out the gloom.

Blue Sundays are horror days for the children; you can't expect them to sit still like older folks. They are full of red blood and active muscles.

Don't make Sunday a day of punishment to your children. They get their cue from you. Don't you be negative and cross and gloomy. It's bad business for you and all the family.

21.

The benefits of walking are so quickly apparent that I hope to get you to make the start and keep it up for two weeks. Then you will require no further urging.

In walking, there are two most important things to do in order to get the greatest benefits: first — walk alone; second — walk your natural gait. So many people tell me they **The Best** would like to walk all, or part of the **Exercise.** way, between their home and office if they had company.

Company is the very thing you don't want in walking, and there are two reasons for this. One is, if you walk with a friend, you will hold your-, self back, or else you will be walking faster than your natural gait. In either case it is a conscious effort, and this conscious effort, to a large degree, will cause you to lose much of the benefit from your walk.

The most important reason, however, is that if you walk with a friend, you are sure to talk, and thus you are using your nervous energy and tiring your brain — the very thing you want to avoid.

Walking gives you physical exercise which is absolutely necessary for health. It is the best exercise I know of, because you do **Walk, Not** not overdo your strength. Walking **Talk.** is beneficial, because when you walk alone, you give your brain a rest. You cannot read the papers, you cannot talk, and your mental apparatus gets complete rest.

I recommend that you walk anywhere from

three to four miles in the morning. If your home is more than four miles from the office, walk three or four miles of the distance and then take the car.

Do not walk home in the evening unless the walk is a short one. In the evening you are tired, and you should conserve your strength. In the morning you are fresh, and the exercises comes to you at a time it is most needed. It will give you strength and courage, and help to keep you in a good mood all day.

I cannot too strongly emphasize the importance of walking alone, for it is then that you shift your nerve energy from the dry cell battery of the brain to the magneto, which is the spinal cord. The spinal cord works automatically andit doesn't wear itself out. The brain tires if it uses its energy.

In walking you use the thought and the brain impulse to start the magneto, and then the spinal cord action is automatic.

This automatic action of the spinal cord is a wise provision of nature to conserve strength.

The spinal cord energy is what you might call automatic habit.

For instance, in dressing and undressing yourself, you will recall that you put on or take off your clothes in regular order without giving the matter any thought. It is just habit.

If you wish to demonstrate the difference between the control of the physical body by brain impulse, and the spinal cord impulse, try this some morning: Start out for your exercise and mentally frame sentences like this as you walk — "right step, left step, right step, left step," and so on. Give thought to each step you have taken, and notice how tired you will be when you have gone half a mile.

The next morning, start to walk naturally; give no thought to walking; keep your mind on the beauties of nature which you are passing, or indulge in pleasant soliloquy, and you will feel no fatigue.

There isn't a bit of theory in this chapter; it is positive, practical sense that I have proved by my own experiences and by the experiences of everyone to whom I have made this suggestion of walking alone.

The moral is this walk every morning and walk ALONE.

22.

The body is made up of billions of little cells. These individual cells are in a state of perpetual activity. They exhaust, wear away, break down with work, and rebuild on food and rest. Every process of life — the beat of the heart, the throb of the brain the thought, the digestion of food, the excretion of waste — all are due to the activity of groups of highly specialized individual cells.

Every cell uses up its own material and throws off poisonous by-products during activity. These by-products, or wastes, are very Body Waste poisonous to the individual cell as well as to the entire organism. To get rid of this waste is one of the first duties of the system.

It is with the body, made up of its countless millions of individual cells, just as it is with a city and its myriad people: the sewage of the community must be collected and disposed of. The city forms its poisons which we call sewage and the body its poisons, which we call excreta (or carbonic acid, urea, uric acid, feces, etc.). It is no more important for a city to gather up and get ride of its poisonous sewage than **Health's Safety** for the ani-mal organism to collect **First.** and excrete its cell-waste. Hence, the importance of maintaining normal and constant elimination throughout the body.

Elimination is kept up by the alimentary tract, the kidneys, the skin, and the lungs. These four are the great pipe-line sewerage systems, so to speak, by which the body throws off its gaseous, liquid and Solidi poisons.

The lungs momentarily strain carbonic acid out of the blood and throw it out in the expired air. They likewise exhale other noxious matters from the system.

The alimentary tract throws off feces, made up of the waste tissue from the whole system, especially the digestive organs, as well as indigestible and non-nutritious portions of the food.

The kidneys strain out urea, uric acid, and certain other poisons from the blood and eject them through the urinary tract.

Finally the skin likewise is an excretory organ and exhales a very definite amount of gaseous and fluid waste in the course of each twenty-four hours.

The skin throws off all the way from a pint totwo quarts of liquid each day in the form of vapor.

Thus, to carry on normal elimination from the body, the breathing, digesting, urinary and cutaneous (skin) systems must be **Proper** kept working normally. To impair **Functioning.** the work of any of these is to retard bodily drainage. To make certain that elimination is going on naturally, it is necessary to secure perfect functioning of lungs, bowels, kidneys and the skin.

Any stoppage in the process of elimination means that some fault has crept into the work of one of these excretory systems. It must be plain now why a disorder of any one of these organs of elimination means so much more profound disturbance to the whole organization than merely disease in one structure. It means that waste products are retained which ought to be thrown out of the body; so straightway every cell in the body begins to be more or less affected. Some poisons disturb one organ more and some another, but in the end the whole body must inevitably be affected.

Lack of exercise, bolting of food, eating soft, starchy things, failure to chew properly, failure to get enough roughage, insufficient water, insufficient fruit — these are the general causes of stoppage in the elimination processes.

Drink one or two glasses of warm water, not hot, the first thing in the morning.

Eat one or two apples, skins and all, every day. Eat toast, especially the crust. Eat cracked wheat or whole wheat bread often.

Exercise plenty. Keep cheerful. Eat regularly.

Very likely you eat too much. You don't need three big meals a day unless you work outdoors at hard physical labor.

Your body is an engine. No use to keep the boiler red hot and two hundred pounds of steam on if your work is light.

Good health depends upon proper assimilation and elimination as nature intended.

Eat less, exercise more, you who work indoors. If you don't use this caution, you are just slowly killing yourself.

23.

Many have the habit of keeping their minds on their weaknesses or their shortcomings. If they read of some one doing a great

Never Say Can't. thing or making a worth-while accomplishment, they say: "I never could do such a thing."

These persons are always saying, "I never have luck. I can't do this. I can't do that."

Always knocking, always thinking "can't" instead of "can" makes for fear, irresoluteness, uncertainty and weakness of character.

To say, "I can't, I haven't the ability, I am unlucky" makes you weak and knocks out all chance for doing things.

Nothing comes out of the brain that wasn't burned in by thought. If you disparage yourself, belittle your capacity, or drown your good impulses with doubt and self-accusation, you are putting away a lot of bad thought in your brain, and no wonder you will lack in initiative, ambition, confidence and courage.

To those who claim to be unlucky, I want to say you are not unlucky — you simply lack pluck.

You start at undertakings with a handicap of fear. You have made up your mind that you can't accomplish. You are half beaten before the game starts. In place of the will to achieve, you approach your task in fear and trepidation. In place of confidence and courage and high aspirations, you set out on your journey with the millstone of doubt and irresolution around your neck.

Confidence And Success. There is but one way to succeed. That is to cast fear and self-accusation aside, and throw your full weight into the struggle with a song on your lips and confidence in your heart. "Victory" should be your battle cry and "Confidence" should be emblazoned on your shield.

Many a man has been whipped in a fight, defeated in a contest, or beaten at an undertaking, but he didn't show it or let the other fellow know it. He just kept on with a brave front, and finally the other fellow quit, mistaking grim determination, pluck and perseverance for strength and victory.

Ethan Allen with his handful of men were asked to surrender by the British general with his superior force. By all the rights and rules of war. Ethan was licked, but he didn't give in, He replied: "Surrender hell; I've just commenced to fight." If Ethan had accused himself and said, "I can't whip that big bunch; there's no hope," he would have been whipped to a finish.

Don't show the enemy or the world your weakness. Don't admit anything impossible that is capable of accomplishment.

It's the "I can" man who wins. No man ever won a fight if he started out by saying, "I can't whip him, he is too much for me; I am no match for him, but I'll try."

No person ever made success in business if he started in with uncertainty, lack of confidence and unbelief in his ability. Confidence has ever been half the battle.

The World's Judgment. Knock yourself, and the world will accept you at your own estimate. Show streaks of yellow cowardice, and the mob will pounceon you like a pack of hungry wolves.

Accuse yourself, curse your luck, belittle your worth, be afraid, and you will remain a mere bump on a log, unnoticed, uninteresting, uninvited.

The world welcomes men who do things. The world judges by outward appearances. If your heart is sick, if your courage is low, don't show it. Put up a stiff attitude and act with confideuce, and that attitude will carry you over many a pitfall and past many an obstacle.

Show strength and the world will help you; show weakness and the world will shun you.

You are prejudiced when it comes to judging yourself. You compare your weakness with your friends' strength, and this comparison is unfair; it makes you lose confidence.

Doubt And Belief. Nothing hurts one worse than doubting one's own ability, assets, and character. When you find yourself experiencing doubt, or inability, or hard luck, turn square around and say: "Be gone, doubt; henceforth I have belief."

Say: "I have ability; I have pluck, and pluck means luck."

Always express confidence, faith, courage, and cheer thoughts, whether you feel them or not. Do this heroically and persistently, and soon the fear shadows and weakness feelings will leave you, and you will be in reality strong, courageous, active, and will do things you never thought possible.

"As a man thinketh, so is he." Always remember that.

Get hold of your thoughts; make yourself think up, and have faith and courage. Hold to your resolve, and the whole world will change. You will prosper, you will have poise, and every once in a while happiness will come as a reward.

No man will be more surprised at your complete change of attitude and character than yourself.

Your problems can only be solved by yourself. Friends can advise, I can suggest, but YOU must act.

Henceforth, never accuse yourself, never feel sorry for your condition or position, cut out fear thoughts,— be strong.

Think faith, courage, cheer, confidence, and strength, and by-and-by the habit will be fixed and natural.

This is as certain truth as I have ever experienced. I know it. I've tried it. I've watched others and the results are always good.

Don't be passive and forget this chapter. Start right this minute to THINK RIGHT.

And you will never regret and never forget this chapter on Self-accusation.

24.

The great colleges turn out thousands of graduates each year, and the great newspapers have much sport ridiculing them in funny pictures. Every great man was once a boy with a dream, and that dream came true because the boy had pep that made him stick to his ambition and kept him from being discouraged because of ridicule or obstacles.

Dare To Dream.

Thomas Carlyle, the poor Scotch tutor, dreamed he wanted to be a great author. His clothes were threadbare, his poverty apparent. Friends taunted and ridiculed him until, goaded to indignation, he cried: "I have better books in me than you have ever read." The crowd laughed incredulously and said: "Poor fellow, he's batty."

Carlyle stuck to his dream and the world has the "History of Frederick the Great" and the "French Revolution" and "Sartor Resartus." When he had finished the manuscript of the "French Revolution," a careless maid built a fire with it. He wasn't discouraged, but went to work and wrote it over again and very likely bet-ter than he wrote it the first time.

Bonaparte in the garden of his military school dreamed of being a great general. He stuck to his dream and he realized his hopes.

Joseph Pulitzer, a poor emigrant, crawled in a cellar way in New York to sleep, and he dreamed of owning a great newspaper. His dream came true, and the newspaper is printed in a building erected on the spot where he dreamed in the cellar way.

Livingston dreamed of exploring darkest Africa; his dream came true.

Edison dreamed of great electrical discoveries. His monument is Menlo Park with its great laboratories.

Ford dreamed of making an automobile for the purse-limited masses — he was jeered; to-day the world cheers him.

My friend, Bert Perrine, was chucked off a stage in the middle of Idaho's great sage brush desert. He said to the driver, "Some day I'll own that stage and I'll use it for a chicken house."

He dreamed and schemed, and to-day the desert is the famous Twin Falls country, blossoming like a rose. And on his beautiful ranch at Blue Lakes, that old stage is used for a chicken house.

Rockefeller dreamed, Lincoln dreamed — so did Garfield, Wilson, Grant, Clay, Webster, Marshall Field, Richard W. Sears and all the other men who have done things worth while in the world.

The great West is the result of dreams come true.

Dream on, my boy; hitch your wagon to a star and stay hitched. That dream and that determination are the things that are to carry you over obstacles, past thorny ways, and through criticism, jeers and ridicule.

Your time will come. Dream and scheme, and make your ideals materialize into living, pulsating realities.

25.

There are many persons who act and advocate ideals merely for effect they are hypocrites.

Here's a little true heart story that probably passed unnoticed except to a very few persons.

Little Spencer Nelson, a poor boy, eight years old, recently died in a hospital with a little bank clasped to his breast. The bank held **Real Charity.** $3.41 in pennies which the boy had saved to buy presents for the poor children in his city.

The little hero had fought manfully through three months' suffering, enduring the torture of five lacerating operations. The pain failed to dim the spirit of unselfishness which burned brightly and clearly in his tired, fever-racked body.

After each operation his mind became more securely fixed on his project to help bring cheer to poor children.

The little savings bank was his companion, and each visitor was asked to contribute to his fund.

Three hours before he died, a smile beautified his thin wasted face as the nurse dropped a dime in his bank. His last Words — a message to his mother — were in a scarcely audible whisper, asking her to remember to use the money to make poor children happy.

That was real charity; that boy had no hypocrisy in his heart.

Seek And You Will Find. The daily paper chronicles instances of sen-sational charity, where men vie with each other to see who can give most and get the most advertising. These men overlook the wonderful opportunities at their door they do not realize the beauti-ful love and charity that would stir in their hearts if they would but look into the out-of-the-way places and get direct connection with pain and buffering.

Little Spencer looked from his cot and saw the suffering of other little children and he wanted to help them, and the very resolve and impulse made him forget his own pain and misery.

In the Book of Good Deeds, the name of Spencer Nelson will be recorded as a sweeter act of charity than any million-dollar gift to a great institution.

What one of you who read these lines can read the story of that little hero and not be touched by the generous love and beautiful con-ception of charity he possessed.

I don't believe much in this far-away charity idea so many have.

Do Good Here At Home. I believe in helping those near where I am rather than sending money to Siam. Poverty and destitution, unhappily, are familiar spectres at home, as elsewhere. He who seeks to do good will not need to range afar. He can find opportunity close at home, near by, where all of us can find it if we only look.

It may be a pleasurable sensation for you to contribute fifty dollars to a missionary scheme in Siam, and get the Missionary report of the budget made up by the committee for the foreign missionary fund.

I know that a bucket of coal in an empty stove, a basket of bread and a liberal hunk of round steak to the starving family around the corner brings the donor a better sensation.

Take a trip to the hospitals, learn about the homes of the suffering patients in the charity ward, and you will resolve it's a better act to send flour to the poor than flowers to the rich.

Little Spencer Nelson had the right idea of charity: definite, immediate help to those he could reach right where he was, rather than sending money to sufferers far, far away.

Let your gifts be principally flour and beef; they help those who need help. Flowers are all right in their place, but there are more places where flour can be used to better purpose.

I'm keener for filling the coffee can of my suf-fering neighbor than filling the coffers of the big charity five thousand miles away.

I try to help both ways, but the home help pays the bigger dividends. What do you think about it?

26.

You have found a friend who has been so much help and comfort to you. I have such a friend too. To-night I am in the mood to think of that friend and write him a letter like this:

This is to You. It is for You. It is about You. You I have in mind and the good influence you have had on me. It is a happiness and **What I** satisfaction to know you, and to **Think of You.** bask in the sunshine of you. The world is better because of you. You have helped to raise the average.

You and your goodness — you do not appreciate what that means. You are so modest, so loath to think of yourself, so thoughtful of others, so unselfish that I must tell you of you and about you.

You have a warm heart that throbs for others' woes and holds sympathy. The great world is cold, selfish, and cares little for others. But you are different; you are a great pillow of rest on which I and others who love you may lay our tired, weary heads, and you wrap your arms of friendship and goodness about us and feel our very heartbeats.

You with your great goodness, **What I** your quiet, sympathetic **Love in You.** understanding — you soothe our troubled spirits and make us glad of you and glad we have the precious privilege of knowing you.

Even now, as I am telling you how I love you, you are trying to wave me aside and stop me, but

I am in the mood and I want to express myself. You know that it is a great sin of omission to refrain from expressing our gratitude for goodness extended to us.

I want to express my gratitude. I do not want to be guilty of the sin of omission.

So here, then, is this little message for you, to tell you that I appreciate you and love you, and these words will last after you are gone and after I am gone, to tell those of to-morrow about you and what those of to-day thought about you.

Your life, your goodness, is an everlasting plant that will flourish in many hearts. Your infence will last beyond the calendar of time; it is indestructible. You have a great credit in the universal bank of good deeds, where you have deposited worth-while acts, deeds, kindnesses, cheer, help, friendship, sympathy, courage, gratitude, and all the most precious jewels of humanity.

I am happy the very moment I think of you. I try to express myself but the feelings and emotions I would describe have not words or sentences to express them. You understand. You are so big in heart, so sensitive in fabric of feeling, so wise in understanding, that I want you to think and feel all the genuine, noble, lovable, appreciative thoughts you can gather together about the one you can most appreciate.

Think hard, sincerely, deeply, about that one, with all your resources of beautiful thought. Think hard that way, and now you will begin to understand my feelings about you, and how I appreciate you.

You, my inspiration, who are so sensitized to feeling, so delicately adjusted to read heart vibrations you must feel this within me that I am trying to express. Not the love between sweethearts, not the love of kin, not the love of friends, but a great universal love I have for you — a love which all who are fortunate enough to know you have for you.

It is a love you cannot return to me in equal measure, because you have not the object in me that can merit such love. That you should love me in the way I love you even in the smallest measure is satisfaction supreme.

It is glorious to know you. You water the good impulses I have; you encourage all that is noble, elevating, and bettering, in me. I shall try to be like you — that is, so far as I can. You are my model; there is but one You. Many may copy you, none may equal you. You are my comfort, you are my joy. A great glorious You that a little 1 am trying to paint a picture of.

How futile my efforts. I might as well try to improve the deep beautiful colors of the morning-glory, or try to retint the lily with a more beautiful white.

And so I bid you good-bye, happy that there is such a one as you in the world — more happy that I know you, and most happy that I know how to appreciate you.

The sum of all good things I can say is, " I love you," and the word " love " I use in its greatest, broadest sense, which covers all the good adjectives.

This is what I think of YOU.

27.

There is a time in the business man's life, between the age of 48 and 52, when he undergoes a pronounced change.

More big men are cut off at 50 than at any other age between 45 and 60.

From 48 to 52 most men change vitally in their physical and mental make-up.

Dangers of Middle Life. Many men hitherto straight, moral men — go to the bad at this time, and per contra, many men quit their immoral and health-hurting habits and change to moral.men. This danger period is when the newly-rich find fault with the wives who have helped them to their success. They grow tired of their wives and seek the companionship of younger women.

The divorce courts give most interesting figures on this point.

At this danger period, men who have been. high livers, voracious eaters and heavy drinkers find themselves victims of diabetes, Bright's disease or other forms of kidney trouble. The country is full of prematurely broken-down men who have failed to heed the danger signals along their way. To persist in self-indulgence is to invite disaster. You must deliberately set about to change your mode of living if you would avoid these shoals on which so many men of middle age have foundered.

Almost every man between 48 and 52 who works indoors, eats too much, exercises too little, sleeps insufficiently.

In this book I have made practical suggestions that have been tried in the furnace of experience and proven adequate. They have helped me; they will help you. They will enable you to gain pep and efficiency; they will give you a new lease on life and make life more worth living.

The Simple Life.

First, live simply; eat simply. If you have in the past, eaten rich foods, drunk fine wines, and have been what the world knows as a "good fellow," your course is clear.

You must call a halt on yourself. This path leads inevitably to the graveyard. Follow the seven simple health suggestions laid down in an earlier chapter, and you will feel better, feel happier and will attack the day's work with vim and vigor.

Avoid undue excitement. Excitement uses up nerve force. It is an energy consumer. Your mind needs repose as well as your body. When you have finished your day's work, leave busi-ness behind you. Do not drag it into your home. In the evening, occupy yourself with a good, worth-while book. Nothing is more conducive to calm and contentment.

Let supper be your one hearty meal of the day. And after supper, play with the kids or joke with your wife; get a smile on your face. When you are home, interest yourself in home con-cerns. The "home men " are the men who live longest. They lead healthy, regular lives, and they keep alive the outside interests that make for peace, poise, content and happiness.

Keep a sharp look-out for tendencies to change your habits and morals.

At 50 you are walking on thin ice; look out, danger is near.

After you are 55, your habits are pretty well established. If you have lived rightly till then, you're safe thereafter and very likely are on your way to a good ripe old age if you take reason-able care of yourself.

28.

We love our own the best; maybe that's why we indulge our own too much. Our duty to our boys;

Our Sons. that's a subject as old as the hills, and it is as important as it is old. It is a subject that has come to the forefront in recent years. Multitudes of paid juvenile workers and sociological experts throughout the country are engaged in the work of keeping the youth of the nation healthily occupied and away from corrupting influences.

Modern conditions have created a "boy problem" which was unknown two generations ago. Then there were no slums reeking with vice and squalor and ugliness. The era of great manufacturing enterprises was just beginning. There were no densely populated cities numbering millions of souls. Amusements were simple. Everywhere were stretches of open country, and boys were allowed to run wild in field and woodland and stream.

The great cities of today have done away with all this. The good, old-fashioned, healthful

Times Have Changed. recreations have disappeared in all but rural communities. In their place has come the lurid "movie" with its tales of crime and violence and passion. At every crowded street corner, vice beckons, and glaring signs lure the curious boy into the vicious cabaret and dancehall.

Today I had the boy problem forcibly presented to me. I saw in a court twenty-four boys who had been brought before the Judge charged with petty crimes. Three were sent to the penitentiary, seven to the reform school and fourteen let go temporarily on good behavior.

A friend of mine interested in criminology tells me the great bulk of hold-ups, thefts, burglaries and murders are committed by boys between 16 and 22 years of age.

These twenty-four boys I mentioned were just ordinary boys, capable of making good citizens if they had had the right kind of home treatment and surroundings. Most of them got in trouble through their association with the "gang " or the "bunch," or the "crowd," and this because daddy didn't have his hand on the rein.

That boy must have companionship; he must have a confidant with whom he can share his joys, his sorrows, his hopes, his ambitions. If the doesn't get this comeraderie at home, he gets it "round the corner."

We know where the boy is when he is at school, but how few of us know the boy's doings between times.

Pool halls tempt the boys, and these resorts are breeding places where filthy stories, criminal slang and evil practices axe hatched.

Pool halls and saloons invite and fascinate the boy. He sees the lights. There is a keen plea-sure in watching the pink-shirted dude with cigarette in his mouth making fancy shots.

There is no one to nag him or bother him; it gets to be his "hang-out," and soon he drifts into a crowd that knows the trail to the red-light district.

Painted fairies dazzle the giddy boy. It takes money to go the pace. Crime is gilded over with slang words. Stealing is called "easy money." Robbery is "turning a trick," and so on.

A boy becomes what he lives on mentally and physically; that's the net of it.

It is a common saying, but a good one, that the boys of today are the men of tomorrow. If you train a boy with care and kindness, he will grow up to be an honest and upright citizen. But let him run a wild, undisciplined course, leave him free to explore the crime-spots and plague-pools of the city, and sooner or later his moral fibre is weakened and ultimately snaps. At best he will become an indifferent citizen; at worst a drifter or a criminal.

There is nothing better for a boy than discipline properly administered. And that brings up the whole matter of army life.

The army is a great maker and developer of men. Boys who were headed for perdition have found in the army a new sense of honor and respect. The rigorous training, the idea of duty, the heroic traditions of the service all these are renewers and rekindlers of manhood. Many a lad who has wasted his health, wealth and substance on the primrose path, has "come back" gloriously in the service of the flag.

The Army: A Maker of Men.

Look at the average soldier or sailor you meet: His skin is tanned by sun and wind to a deep brown. His eyes are crystal clear. There is youth and strength in his tread. There he stands, clean as a whistle. No fat, no flabbiness just solid sinew and ruddy health. He is a living exponent of what military training can do for every boy in the country.

Hard work, strength-building exercises, sufficient sleep, regular hours, simple, wholesome food, systematic training — these are the things the army and navy offers. And these are the things that make real men.

But no training that school or church or army can give him relieves you, Dad, of your obligation to the boy. In the last analysis, it is your influence that will either make him or break him, for it is to you that he looks for guidance and comradeship in his most impressionable years.

If you are his chum, if sister shares his amusements with him, if the family work and live on the "all for one and one for all" basis, if the boy is kept busy and interested, he can be easily trained.

Neglect him and he will neglect you. Love him and he will love you. Meet him halfway, he's

Be Worth Copying.

impressionable. Show him a kindness, he will respond. Show him a good example, he will follow. You have to be with him, or know where he is every minute.

During his period of adolescence, say from twelve or thirteen years to sixteen or seventeen, that boy is a mass of plaster of paris, easily shaped while plastic, but once set, all but impossible to recast

That's the time, Dad, you must be on YOUR job with your boy.

Your counsel, example, love, interest and teaching will MAKE the boy.

Think of these things, Dad, and think hard, and think hard NOW. Tomorrow may be too late.

29.

Our daughters how much we love them!

How happy we are to have their fresh, smiling faces about us! Their girlish laughter lightens our home hours and creates an atmosphere of joy.

Our Daughters. What would we not give if we could but insure their happiness! Our fondest and most cherished hopes are bound up in them as they grow up under our eyes and blossom into womanhood.

Girl, what a wonderful creature you can be. What a glorious success you can make of your life if you get the right start, find the right hands to help you, the right hearts to love you, and the right eyes to watch you, the right thoughts to make you, and the right ideals to guide you.

There are so many influences to spoil you —so much convention, so much artificiality, so much snobbery, so much caste, so much foolish frivolity.

Then there are the wrong examples, the wrong grooming, the wrong environments, the wrong influences surrounding you. Really, it is not to be wondered at why so many girls lose their heads and make a fizzle of their young lives.

The fizzle is generally made because daddy and mama have a lot of foolish notions about bringing up girls. Especially is this so if the parents are wealthy.

Here is the history of many a rich girl: She is born without welcome, fed on a bottle, reared by a nurse, grows up in a nursery, becomes estranged from her mother; later on, she is sent away to school, mixes with a lot of other rich girls,

The Wrong Way. gets lots of foolish notions, false estimates, and prejudiced views. She graduates and comes home, and then, to commemorate the event, there are a lot of "doings " which she attends. Following this is the show-off, which is called a debut.

She is exhibited like a filly at the horse show, and some high-collared young man wins her head, although she thinks it's her heart. She believes it is the proper time for her to marry, and he is such "a swell fellow," he is such "good company," and he "dances so well " — these qualities win her heady

So the girl marries and has children; the husband goes broke, and the girl awakens to the necessity of coming down from her pedestal, facing stern necessity, and raising her children as her mother should have raised her.

That's the picture of the poor rich girl whose parents are to blame for the nonsense she crammed into her head.

But, you, Girl — you are going to learn your cooking on a gas range instead of a chafing dish; you'll learn to bake bread before fudge; you'll learn how to cook solids before you learn to make salads.

You will combine simplicity, sentiment, sense, sereneness, sweetness, rather than envy, frills, feathers and foolishness.

God's noblest calling for woman is the raising of children and the founding of a home.

To cook and sew is a higher duty and better occupation than bridge parties and society. Not

that you must cook and sew, my dear, but that you should be able to in case the need should
Cooking and Sewing. arise. With the ability to cook and sew, you can properly direct the cook or seamstress, and they will respect you for your education.

I want you to be golden girls — girls who love home and children; girls who love simple things, natural things. I want you to be sweet rather than pretty, lovable rather than popular.

Do not look upon matrimony as a means to provide food and finery for yourself.

Do not be ashamed of an old-fashioned mother. Do not be a "good fellow." Do not be afraid to say, "I can't afford it."

Help the family. Be part of it, and not apart from it.

When you are old enough to have a beau, do not be afraid to bring him into your home, no matter how humble it is.

Do not esteem your boy friends for the amount of money they spend on your entertainment. Happiness does not consist of lobster-suppers and taxi-rides to the theatre. Ten cents will bring just as much real happiness as ten dollars spent for mere display.

Be modest, girls; it is your greatest asset.

Don't gossip or belittle other girls. Find the good you can say of others; that quality makes you more attractive.

Watch out for candied words and flattery; these things mark the hypocrite, and a hypocrite is an abomination. Flattery is a practiced deceit — a dishonorable bait to catch affections.

Do not allow any young man to relate a story

in your presence that has the slightest risque turn to it.

Show by your words and your actions that such presumption is an insult.

Be square with yourself; be square to the man who is after your heart. Put yourself **The Right** mentally in the place of a wife when **Man.** a man gets serious.

Don't hurry, girls; don't judge the man by his money prospects but by his character and ambition. Have nothing to do with any young suitor who isn't always kind, considerate and attentive to his mother. And when real love comes to you and you decide to marry, marry a man of character who courts you in the sweet, simple, old way.

If a young man spends money extravagantly before marriage, hard times will always be around during his married life.

The most precious possessions in the world are happiness and love, and these come from simple things, genuineness, and usefulness.

The painted, powdered, tinsel, fluff, feathers and furbelow girl may be a dashing creature now, and you may envy her, but you, with your quiet, sweet, simple, sensible ways — you will win real love, real respect, real affection, real pleasures, real satisfaction, in all the days to come; you will make a success of your life.

Frills and feathers may have an attraction for the girl who makes a fizzle of her life, but sweetness and simplicity, sentiment and sense, are precious jewels that will endure for all time.

The world is full of new-fashioned, slangy, dancy, fancy, foolish girls who marry for style, stunts and society, and their married life is failure, worry and regret.

The Road to Unhappiness. They do not realize, poor things, until it is too late, that money and luxury are not enough to bring happiness. When this truth comes home to them, there is nothing left but disillusion, heartache and sorrow.

Be the golden, pure, old-fashioned, sweet, simple, quiet, modest girl who knows things, rather than one who is a show-off girl.

When the right young man comes along, he will recognize the kind of girl you are when he meets you. He will see in you a girl of pure gold; a sweet, natural, sensible girl, who will be a helpmate to him and not a drawback.

So then, here is the hope that you, girl, will start right, keep right, and end right. I want you to think of sense, sentiment, and simplicity rather than dances, dollars, duds and doings.

I want your life to be one of poise, happiness and serenity instead of noise, worry and nerves.

This little message is all for you — GIRL.

30.

Many churches today are running to extremes in one way or another.

On the one hand, they are conducted along the lines of form, ceremony and ritualism; the other extreme results in excitement, ecstasy and fanaticism.

The church of forms, rituals and ceremonies attracts the passive who are willing to let the priest or pastor or prelate take charge of the religious work while they, the **Real Religion.** attendants or worshippers, sit quietly by and say " amen " and join in the responses.

Paul said, "Away with those forms." Christ, in ministering to humanity, gave no forms and made no set sentences for his followers. The Lord's Prayer was given with the admonition, "After this manner pray ye," and certainly not with the command, "Pray ye with these words."

Form, ceremony and ritual are much like most associated charities — a sort of convention. Forms cannot express the deep emotions, the natural longings, or the human desires; they are echoes, hollow and unsatisfying.

For those who do not feel, for those who do not act, for those who belong to churches because of convention, or for social reasons, forms and frills fill the bill.

Form is an exterior religion, an outward show. Form doesn't touch the heart or awaken the soul. Form in religion is like a formal dinner. It is a gaudy display rather than a plan to satisfy hu-man heart hunger.

Opposite to formal religion is the frenzied "scare-you-to-death" excitement method, which relies upon mental intoxication to **Scare-You-to-Death Method.** stir the people. Like other forms of intoxication, the effect soon wears off.

I have little patience or sympathy for the business men who hire professional evangelists to come to town to start revivals. The sensational revivalists have too acute an appreciation of the dollar to convince me of their sincerity in their work.

A laborer is worthy of his hire, and a preacher, teacher or benefactor of any sort should be well paid. But when I see these big guns taking away from ten to one hundred thousand dollars in cold cash for a three weeks' campaign converting the poor suffering people, the thought comes to me that if the evangelist were sincere, he would buy a lot of bread, coal and underwear, and hire a lot of trained nurses with a big part of that money.,

Christ and his Apostles were of the people; they worked with and among the people; they had no committees, no guarantees and no business men's subscription lists.

It's mighty hard to read about these sensational evangelists taking in thousands of dollars for a couple of weeks' revival meetings, and harmonize that religion with the religion of Christ, the carpenter, and his Apostles, who were fishermen and workmen.

The exciting, intoxicating, **How They Do It.** frenzied revival method is pretty much the same in its working wherever it is practised. The evangelist starts in with the song,

"Where is My Wandering Boy Tonight;" then follows the picture of mother, which is painted with sobs of blood. Then follows mother's deathbed scene until the audience is in tears. Gesticulation, mimicry, acting, sensationalism, slang and weepy stories follow, until the ferment of excitement is developed to a high pitch, and droves flock down the sawdust trail to be made over on the instant into sanctified beings.

The evangelist stays until his engagement is up, and then departs with a pocket full of nice fat bank drafts.

But there is nothing new about this method.

It is as old as humanity. It is the same method that is practised in the more remote and

An Old-Time Method.
uncivilized portions of the world today, where garishly painted savages congregate and render homage to their gods in an orgy of yelling, whooping and beating of the tom-tom.

It is a sad commentary on the established profession of the ministry that sensational professionals are called in and paid fabulous prices to convert the people in their community.

I do not take much stock in either the frigid form-and-ceremonial method with its frills, or the frenzied fire-and-brimstone, scare-you-to-it extreme.

Somewhere between these extremes is the rational, natural, sane road to travel the religion of brotherly love; of cheers, not tears; of hope, not fear; of courage, not weakness; of joy, not sorrow; of help, not hindrance.

The religion that makes us love one another here — not the kind that says we shall know each other there; the religion that has to do with human passions, human trials, human needs, instead of the frigid form or the fevered frenzy; the religion that avoids the extremes of heat and cold — that's the kind the world needs most.

Christ taught love, kindness, charity. He spoke not of beautiful churches and opera-singing choirs. He spoke not of robes, vestments, forms or rituals.

The Religion of Love.

One of the most beautiful things in the Bible is the story of the good Samaritan with his simple, unostentatious aid to a wounded man — a man whom the Samaritan knew as an enemy of his people, but who was none the less a brother. And you will remember how the priest of the temple — the man who taught charity and love — drew up his skirts and passed the wounded man by.

31.

Patriotism — one's love for one's country — is a natural and a beautiful sentiment. With the spirit of idealism behind it, it becomes one of the noblest sentiments that has been developed in the course of humanity's long upward

Love of Country.

march to civilization.

Today, on Europe's battlefields, millions of men are hazarding their lives. They do so gladly, willingly, with a firm and reasoned conviction in the justice of the cause for which they fight. That is intelligent patriotism — the kind of patriotism that is based on understanding and knowledge.

But the world to-day is conscious that there is another kind of patriotism — a false patriotism that is fostered and fomented by ambitious governments for purposes of aggression and aggrandizement.

This false patriotism is not a free or voluntary thing. It is the blind, instinctive feeling of sheeplike men who have been bred beneath the yoke of servility and obedience and are like clay in the hands of their overlords. They know not why they fight, but through fear or intimidation or force, they slavishly submit to the will of their Kaiser or Emperor and his minions.

This great war, and most every great war of the past, was made possible by a distorted understanding of patriotism. This false patriotism is one of the narrowest and most cruel forces in the world, and when linked with militarism, it becomes the most dangerous. It causes wars, waste and desolation. It creates jealousies, inspires jingoism and braggadocio, keeps alive the fight spirit, and menaces the peace and security of nations.

Militarism. Militaristic rulers, fired by selfish egotism, know full well what a powerful force patriotism is, and they nurse the babes with fatherland stuff and give them tin soldiers to play with and tin helmets to wear.

Patriotism, when it reflects love of the place of one's nativity, when it is based on home ties and associations, is a beautiful and touching thing. But when unscrupulous autocrats utilize this sentiment for their own aggressive purposes, it becomes a menace that must be put down if other nations are to enjoy the blessings of peace and liberty.

False Patriotism A Menace. To keep this false patriotism alive, wars must be made, so that human blood can be secured to keep the monster from famishing. And so, on slight pretexts, or no pretexts at all, the war lords and imperial autocrats rattle their swords in their scabbards and let loose the avalanche of war on the world.

Such patriotism is failure and worse than failure. It is a reversion to the brute age of mankind. It flings a moral challenge to the world that the world must either accept or perish.

So much for this monstrous perversion of Right and Reason that has turned Europe into a shambles, and has banded the civilized nations of the world together in a mighty struggle for freedom and democracy.

True patriotism is one of the world's constructive forces. It overleaps national frontiers, and is inspired by the ideals of international peace, good-will and amity. It looks forward to the time when national barriers will be let down, and the brotherhood of man will be recognized the world over.

Such patriotism is the patriotism of Right Makes Might — not Might Makes Right. It is the kind of patriotism that prevails only among the free, democratic, peace-loving peoples of the world who are fighting to-day for the preservation of free institutions and the rights of humanity.

The opposite sort of patriotism is the autocratic, militaristic kind that has furnished the world with an example of savage ferocity and vindictive cruelty that it will not soon forget.

In this great struggle, we see Democracy ranged against Autocracy, Right against Might, True Patriotism against False Patriotism. The Right will triumph, as it always has, when pitted against the forces of hate, greed and reaction.

32.

Danger lies in extremes. Too much of any-thing is bad for the human being's health. There is a certain comfortable proportion of exercise and rest which, when mixed **The Happy** together, will give bodily efficiency. **Medium.** Too much exercise is bad, too little is bad.

Until recent years, our vocations and the habit of going to or from our places of business gave, us a well-balanced amount of exercise, rest, work and pleasure, and all went well.

Lately, we hear much about worry, neurasthenia, nervous prostration and the like. There are several contributing causes to the mental and physical ills which are caused by "nerves."

First of all, we have an epidemic of labor-saving devices. The principal argument used by the manufacturer of a labor-saving device is, "It makes money and saves work." Making money and getting soft snaps seem to be the objectives of most human beings.

The labor-saving devices take away exercise.

The machine does the work. The artisan simply feeds the hopper, puts in a new roll, or drops in the material. He sits down and watches the wheels go around, likely smoking a cigarette in the meanwhile, and more than likely reading **Changed** the sporting sheet of a yellow **Conditions** newspaper. **of Work.** Possibly few of my readers have given the matter serious thought, and they will be astounded at the changed conditions of work which have come into our modern life. It will be interesting to note here some of these changes.

Men used to live within walking distance of their work. Now the electric street railway and the speedy automobile have eliminated the necessity for much walking.

Men used to climb stairs. The elevator has now so accustomed us to the conveniences that stairs are taboo.

Machines have replaced muscles. The old printer walked from case to case and got exercise. Today he sits in an easy backed chair and uses a linotype.

Telephoning is quicker than traveling. No one "runs for a doctor."

Our houses have electric washers, electric irons and many other labor-saving devices.

Even the farmer has his telephone, his auto, his riding plow, his milking machine and his cream separator.

In the stores, the cash boy has disappeared. The cash carrier takes the money to a girl who sits in the office, a machine makes the change, and another machine does her mathematics.

Perils of Inactivity. The modern idea of efficiency puts a premium on the sedentary feature of occupations, and employes are frequently automatons that sit. The business man sits at his desk, sits in a comfortable automobile as he goes home, sits at the dinner table and sits all evening at the theater, or at the card table. It is sit, sit, sit until he gets a big abdomen, a puffy skin and a bad liver.

He tries to counteract this with forced exercise in a gymnasium or a couple of hours golfing a week. Very likely, his golfing is more interesting because of the side bets than because of the exercise.

We are losing out on the natural, pleasurable, and practical exercises, mixed in the right proportions to promote physical poise and health. Things are too easy, luxury and comfort too teasing, for the ordinary mortal to resist, and the great mob sits or rides hundreds of times when they should stand or walk.

When my objective point is five or six blocks, I walk, and I think on the way. I probably get in from two to four miles of walking every day, which my friends would save by riding in the street cars or autos.

I walk to my office every morning — a distance of nearly four miles.

I walk alone, so that I may relax and not expend conscious effort as is the case when I walk with another.

That morning walk prevents me from reading slush and worthless news, and relieves me of the necessity of talking and using up nerve energy.

I get the worth-while news from my paper by the headlines and by trained ability to separate the wheat from the chaff.

Four Great Body-Builders. I just feel fine all the time, and it's because I get to bed early, sleep plenty, exercise naturally, think properly and get the four great body-builders in plenty: air, water, sunshine, food; and, the other four great health-builders, which are : good thought, good exercise, good rest, and good cheer.

The great crowd aims at ease, and so the business man sits and loses out on the exercise 'his body and mind must have. And therefore the great crowd pays tribute to doctors, sanitarium, rest cures, fake tonics, worthless medicines, freakish diet fads, and crazy cults, isms, and discoveries that claim to bring health by the easy, lazy, comfortable sitting route.

Believe me, dear reader, it is not in the cards to play the game of health that way. "There ain't no sich animal" said the ruben as he saw the giraffe in the circus, and likewise, there "aint no sich thing" as health and happiness for the man who persistently antagonizes Nature, and hunts ease where exercise is demanded.

The law of compensation is inexorable in its demand that you have to pay for what you get and that you can't get worth-while things by worthless plans.

You must exercise enough to balance things, to clear the system, to preserve your strength; it doesn't take much time.

33.

This afternoon I am sitting on a glacial rock in the forest at the foot of Mount Shasta. A beau-tiful spot in which to rest and a glorious page from the book of nature to read.

A canopy of deepest blue sky above, with sunshine unstopped by clouds. The rays of old Sol pulsate themselves into an endless variety of flowers, plants **Back to** and vegetable life which Mother **Nature.** Earth has given birth to. Glorious trees of magnificent size reach up into the blue and give us shade. Ozone sweeps gently through the forest, impregnated with the perfume of fir, balsam, cedar, pine and flowers.

In this spot, nature has thrown up mountains of volcanic rock, which hold the winter's snow in everlasting supply to quench the thirst of plant, of animal, and of the millions of humans in the lower country.

The whole hillside around me is a community of springs of crystal water laden with iron and precious salts. It is the breast of Mother Earth which nurses her offspring.

Here are no noises of the street; the newsboy's cry of "extra" is not heard. The raucous voice of the peddler, the din of trucks, the honk of automobiles, the clatter of the city — all these are absent.

There is no noise here — just the sweet music of falling water, and the Aeolian (Greek God Of Winds) lullaby made by the breeze playing on the pine needles.

My eyes take in a panorama of beautiful nature in colors and contrasts that would give stage fright to any artist who tried to paint the scenes on canvas.

I am getting pep. This is my treatment for tired nerves; 'tis the "medcin' of the hills;" 'tis nature's cure, and how it brings the pill box **Gaining Pep.** and the bottle of tonic into contempt! I'm letting down the high tension voltage and getting the calm, natural pulsation that nature intended the human machine to have.

So quiet, so peaceful, so natural is the view that I drink in inspiration of a worth-while kind. No war news to read, no records of tragedy, no degrading chronicles of man's passions, of man's meanness and man's selfishness.

A little chipmunk sits upright on a rock before me wondering at the movements of my yellow pencil and the black mark it makes on the paper.

A delicate lace-winged insect lights on my tablet, and a saucy " camp robber," or mutton bird, wonders at the unusual sight of me, the big man animal brother. A big beetle is getting his provisions for the winter. I recognize his occupation, for I've read about him in Fabre's wonderful books on insect life. ("Poet of Science" – see efabre.net)

Here, in the sanctum sanctorum of the forest, I am made a member of Nature's lodge, and the **Nature's Lodge.** ants and bugs and beetles and flowers and plants and trees are initiating me and telling me the secrets of the order. I can only tell you, who are in the great busy world outside, the lessons and morals. The real secrets I must not tell; you will receive them when you, too, come to the hills and forests, and sit down on a rock alone and go through the initiation.

You are invited to come in; your application is approved, and you are eligible to membership.

Come to Nature's lodge-meeting and clear away the cobwebs from your weary brain; get inspira-tion and be a man again.

Come — soothe and rest and build up those shredded, weakened, tired, weary nerves. Let the sun put its coat of health on you, and let the ozone put the red blood of strength in your veins.

Come and get perfect brain and body-resting sleep. Come to this wonderful, happy, helpful lodge and get a store of energy, and an abundance of vital ammunition

Rest and Recreate.

with which to make the fight, when you go back to your factory or office. The doctor can lance the carbuncle, but Nature's outdoor medicine will prevent your having a carbuncle.

The doctor can stop a pain with a poison drug, but Nature's outdoor medicine will prevent your having the disorder which makes the pain.

No, brother, you can't get health out of a bottle or a pill box. But you can get it from Mother Nature's laboratory, where she compounds air, water, sunshine, beauty, music, thought; where she gives you exercise and rest, health, happiness, all summed up into cashable assets for the human in the shape of poise, efficiency and peace.

34.

Mother, you are the one person in all the world whose kindness was never the preface to a request. That's the sweetest tribute we can pay you, and the most truthful one. It covers devotion, love, sentiment, motherhood, and all the noble attributes that go to make the word "Mother" the most hallowed, most sacred, most beautiful word in the English language.

Mother.

There are not words or sentences that can express to you what we think of you or convey our appreciation of you.

You want our love; you have it. You should be told of our love; we tell you. Appreciation and gratitude are payments on account, but with all our appreciation and with our whole life's gratitude, the debt we are under can never be paid.

"We have careful words for the stranger,
And smiles for the sometime guest
But oft to our own the bitter tone,
Though we love our own the best."

We've hurt you, Mother, many times, by our thoughtlessness and by the resentment we felt over your plans and your views about the things we did, and you have had heartaches because of such actions of ours.

The Mother Love.

Forgive us, Mother, we're sorry. And there you are, dear; the moment we ask your forgiveness, your great, tender, loving heart has forgiven us and erased the marksof transgression. Always thinking of us, always excusing us, always doing for us, always watching us and always loving us in the most unselfish way.

We love you, Mother; we appreciate you. We are going to show our appreciation and love so much more from now on. We have just come to our senses and realized what a wonderful, necessary, helpful being you are.

Your sweetness, your gentleness, your goodness, your love, are parts of you. They all go to make up that word "Mother."

Your life, your acts, your example, your Motherhood, have all helped the world so much more than you will ever know.

In the everlasting record of good deeds, your name is in gold.

In the everlasting memory of those who appreciate you, your face, your life, is a sacred, helpful picture that grows more beautiful as the days pass.

In tenderness, in appreciation, in love, let us dedicate these thoughts and voice these expressions to Mother, who gives her life by inches, and who would give it all on the instant for her children, if necessity called for the sacrifice.

How feeble are words when we try to describe Mother!

35.

This is your inning, Dad.

There have been so many beautiful things written about Mother and all the rest of the family that it is high time we should tell you how much we love you and how much we appreciate you.

Just Dad.

You've worked so hard; you've been so ambitious to do things for your loved ones, and they have accepted your sacrifice and work and watchfulness as matter of fact.

You've had dreams of a some day when you would relax and play and enjoy, but you have set that some day too far ahead. You consider yourself only after all your loved ones are comfortable and happy, and time is passing, Dad.

You are too unselfish, too much centered in that some day. Let's change things a bit, Dad. Some-times the "some day" doesn't come.

You are entitled to happiness and pleasure and health and joy right here, now, to-day. It's your duty to have them.

Your loved ones do not want you to spend your health in getting wealth. They don't want to see you wornout, tired, weary and unhappy, in the evening of your life. Besides it's your duty to let them share the responsibility, and work out their own problems. They will be better equipped for life after you are gone if you let them gain knowledge by practical experience.

Come on, Dad; get in the group and enjoy things now and you will live longer, and get more out of life, and give more pleasure to your loved ones. Get in the game, Dad; let's see the old light and twinkle in your eyes; let's have the sunshine on your face; the lovelight on your lips, and the happiness in your heart.

Keep Alive The Spirit of Youth.

Leave your cares at the office; prepare your mind for play, and you will feel so much better and stronger and so much more successful in your business.

We don't want to hear any more sh-h-h — sh-h-h — or whispers when you come home. We don't want to feel that uncomfortable feeling of restraint; let's laugh and sing and love and play — let's make your home-coming a joyous event.

We all love you, Dad, but you haven't made it as comfortable as you might for us when we try to express our love. You've been too tired, too busy, too much occupied with those business thoughts.

Don't you see how we love you and how we appreciate you? Don't you know that there is no one in the world who can take the place of Dad?

Keep your heart young, Dad; we will help it you only say, "Come on." We are waiting for the signal. Let's start the new schedule tonight. Come on, Dad, what do you say?

36.

We speak of the three kingdoms: the animal, the vegetable and the mineral kingdoms, and **What Our** every substance is classified into **Bodies are** one of these. The exact truth is **Composed Of.** there is but one kingdom, which is the mineral. The vegetable substances and animal combinations are made of mineral elements.

In a rough way we distinguish the mineral kingdom as those substances called elements, such as iron, sulphur, carbon, oxygen, hydrogen, sodium and the like.

These elements are unchangeable in themselves; they do not grow. The animal is made of mineral elements associated in certain proportions, such as albumin, carbon, lime, water, salt and the like. The vegetable kingdom also consists of these various chemical combinations.

Seed, when planted, extracts the minerals from the air and the earth and combines them into a plant, which grows and has for its object the making of seeds to reproduce and perpetuate itself.

The plant has life, but it has no spiritual or mental equipment, and therein vegetable life differs from the animal life. The animal eats vegetable and animal flesh. Through the vegetable he gets the mineral matter necessary for body-building. He also gets a plentiful supply of mineral from the flesh he eats, which flesh was first built up through the vegetables the animal ate.

These are definite facts.

The human body may be analyzed and separated into something like a dozen substances, among which are water, which is three-fourths of the body's structure, carbon, lime, phosphorus, iron, potassium, salt and so on.

By reading a book on anatomy you can learn just exactly the proportions of the substances in the human body.

What Our Bodies Need. All these chemicals are formed in the shape of little cells, myriads of which are in the body. These cells are constantly being destroyed and new ones made to take their place.

Parts of the body are replaced every twenty-four hours; other parts less often.

Scientists tell us that the whole body is replaced every seven years. Every move you make destroys cells which nature has to replace. Isn't it reasonable then to conclude that if a man should fail to eat enough lime for his bodybuilding, his bones would suffer? If he does not get enough iron, his blood will suffer, and so on. I am convinced that most physical ailments are caused by a deficiency of the mineral elements in the body.

Phosphorus and potash are necessary to human welfare. These elements are in the husk of the wheat, and when the husk is taken off in making flour, the resulting product is mostly starch. The person who lives mostly on white bread will suffer from lack of phosphorus and potash.

Nothing could be better for the health of the American people than the nationwide food campaigns the government is conducting. The educational value of these campaigns is enormous.

Eat less wheat! White bread is unessential. Bran, or whole wheat bread, is far more healthful and nourishing, and contains more of the elements the human body needs.

Eat more fruit. People do not eat enough fruit. Every year thousands of bushels of peaches and grapes and other fruit go to waste because the demand is not great enough to ship the entire output to the great consuming centers.

Study your body's needs. Health is maintained at its proper level only so long as you eat carefully and wisely.

37.

The practice of medicine in the past has been directed towards the curing of disease and physical ailments already developed. The practice of medicine in the future is to be along preventive lines. Science is showing us how to prevent infection. Science is fighting the deadly microbe which comes to us in the air we breathe, the water we drink, and the food we eat, and the infected things we touch.

The Why of Disease. Nature has supplied the human body with a home guard of necessary bacteria, and in the circulation system are phagocytes which fight the invading microbes and generally destroy them. When the system is weakened through disease, through lack of exercise, or through improper food, disease has an easy time.

I want you to remember this golden prescription It is composed of the following: Good Air, Good Water, Good Sunshine, Good Food, Good Exercise, Good Cheer, Good Rest and Good Thought. If you take this golden prescription,you will make of yourself a giant in brain and brawn strength.

You can't get health out of a bottle. You can't get the system to absorb iron if you take it in the form of tincture of iron. You can eat a pound of rust, which is oxide of iron, and none of that iron will be absorbed in the system.

What to Eat. As I have explained in another chapter, you must take the mineral in the system through the vegetable route. You will get iron that will be assimilated when you eat beefsteak. Beefsteak has blood; the blood has iron. You will also get iron when you eat spinach.

Fads, Cults, Isms. Every element necessary for your body is found in some vegetable or animal food; therefore, you should refrain from confining yourself to a very few articles of food.

Don't pay any attention to the faddist who gives you a rigorous diet or unpalatable food. You simply make yourself miserable, and you generate more worry and unhappiness by your discipline than the good you get from these freak fads. There are a thousand different fads and cults and isms, each one claiming to be right. Probably each one contains a small portion of right. But it is a sure thing that The Right is too big a thing to be confined within narrow formulae and creeds.

We all eat too much meat, but that a strict vegetarian diet is the necessary thing for good health I deny. The sheep, the cow, and horse are vegetarians, and they are short lived. The eagle, the lion, the man, eat animal food, and they are long lived.

I may be prejudiced, but it does seem to me that the strict vegetarians are a skinny, sallow-looking lot of humans, speaking generally. I do find that the healthier specimens of vegetarians are those who eat plenty of eggs and drink plenty of milk, both of which are animal food, and both of which have nearly all the elements necessary to sustain life.

I don't like fads in the matter of eating. The amount a person consumes should be in exact accord with the body's requirements neither more nor less.

The human body is a machine from a food standpoint. It is an engine that has work to do, and accordingly the amount of fuel necessary for the engine should be in proportion to the amount of work that the engine is called on to perform.

The majority of city-dwelling people eat too much. This is especially true of men in sedentary occupations, and women whose household duties are light. If your engine needs twenty pounds of steam, how foolish it is to keep up a hundred pounds pressure! If you had five-horsepower work to perform, how foolish it would be to install a two-hundred-and-fifty-pound engine!

Eat Less, Exercise More.

Eat less of everything. Fat and flabbiness and over-feeding is a national vice with us. The fashionable cafés and restaurants are thronged with puffy, heavy-jowled men and women, eating and drinking. Hotels and food-purveyors are constantly inventing new palate tickling dishes to tempt your appetite. Orchestras and dramatic troupes are engaged to entertain and amuse you while you overload your stomach, take on fat, and lay the foundation for future cases of indigestion or dyspepsia.

There is no escaping a day of reckoning for such mistreatment of yourself. If you would keep yourself fit, it is important that you eat only what is necessary to maintain yourself at normal weight and strength.

You do not often find dyspepsia or indigestion among men or women who work hard physically.

Isn't it reasonable to suppose that this is because they work hard?

You who work indoors, with little physical exercise, will find wonderful benefits if you will cut down the fuel.

Much of the physical trouble comes from filling up the boiler too much.

Cut down the food and you will feel better.

38.

Anger and revenge are great pull-backs to health.

Anger makes the blood rush to the head, weakens the body, and distorts the vision.

Anger And Poise.

When a woman gets angry, she quarrels with her lover, her husband or her children. Any one of these things is a calamity.

When a man gets angry, he is a wild man. His eyes glitter, his mouth is cruel, his fists clinch, his body trembles, his blood veins strain, and he does more harm to his system in five minutes of anger than nature can repair in a day.

Anger makes weak stomachs, dizzy heads, poor judgment, lost friends, despair and sickness, and if the habit becomes confirmed, will likely lead to apoplexy (stroke). When two men have differences, watch the cool man finish victor; the angry man always loses. Keep your head; let the other fellow fret and fume.

He will tie himself up in a knot, and when the gong is rung, he will be the loser.

Serenity is one of God's blessings. Fortunate is the man who can hold his serenity.

When you get a letter that stirs you to anger, don't answer that letter for forty-eight hours; then write a moderately vitriolic letter — and then tear it up.

The Futility of Revenge.

I know you are tempted and goaded, and your limit of endurance is sometimes reached. But I know that revenge is sweet only in anticipation. I know that revenge by anger and by the cruel "eye for an eye" measure is never, never sweet.

I have been the victim of imposition, ingratitude and insincerity, and advantage has been taken of me because I kept my poise and serenity.

I have been called easy, and soft, and friends have shown me where I was imposed upon, but I was stooping to conquer. I kept my reserve, my resistance, and my power ready until time, place, and preparedness let me spring my coup, and then I cashed in beautifully in principal and interest for those acts and hurts.

I have power now in my hands to make others suffer keenly and deeply for wrongs they have done me. Yet I do not exercise that power to revenge.

I have been misjudged and misunderstood, because cowardly persons have lied and villified me, and have accused me of motives and acts of which I was innocent.

I am well hated now by one person in particular, who blames me for things another is guilty of. A word from me would clear myself, but it would bring gloom and despair to that person and would not make me any more cognizant of my innocence.

Time somehow will bring out the truth; the cowardly, guilty individual who basks in the favor of the one who is angry at me will **Time, The** surely pay for his wrong. This I **Arbiter.** know, and I am satisfied with the ultimate result.

My former friend, who is angry at me, would simply switch the anger current to the guilty one if I told the facts; the guilty person couldn't stand that anger like I can. My act would break up a home and bring misery. The satisfaction I would receive would not equal the sorrow my act would cause to others.

I am far removed from the location where these people live, and I can stand the anger of the one who puts the blame on me by accepting the lies of another as truth.

I have the documents in black and white, yet I don't use them because I have poise and the consciousness of knowing I am right, and those who are dear to me know it, too.

I've tried both plans, the plan of anger and the plan of poise, and I like poise better.

I believe I hear more birds, I believe I get more pleasure out of life and living than the man who gets angry and loves revenge.

Anyway, I <u>think</u> so, and "as a man thinketh in his heart, so is he."

39.

Sleeping, like breathing and digesting, is controlled by the subconscious brain centers. Natural sleep requires no positive mental impulse; it's just relaxing, and nature takes care of the process.

That is natural sleep, but when you start your dry cell battery, the brain, and commence to worry and fear, you are going to stay awake. Then the conscious mind dominates the **Can't Sleep.** subconscious mind, and you banish the very comforter you seek to woo.

Business men who work under high tension all day on business matters, and high tension all evening in threshing over again the business of the day, are almost sure to suffer from insomnia.

The continuance of this habit of thinking of business day and night brings on the insomnia habit and that, in turn, gives rise to the delusion that you are fighting for your natural sleep. This produces worry, the demon that kills and maims.

To have an occasional wakeful night is natural; it is an evidence of intelligence: the mental dullard never has wakeful nights.

Unless the fear of sleeplessness becomes a full grown phobia, no anxiety need be felt. The fear of insomnia, the over-anxiety to go to sleep, is to be more dreaded than insomnia itself.

To get refreshing sleep you must **To Get** put yourself in a state of actual **Results.** physical tiredness. Take exercise. Walk in one direction until the first symptoms of becoming tired appear, then walk home. Take a hot bath, then sponge with cold or cool water. Put a cold cloth at the head, and rub the backbone with cold water.

Open your windows wide, then relax. Don't worry; you are going to sleep.

Lie on your back, open your eyes wide, look up as if you were trying to see your eyebrows, hold your eyes open this way ten to twenty seconds, then close them slowly. Repeat this several times.

Sleep will have descended on you before you realize it.

Or occupy your mind with auto-suggestions like this: "I am going to sleep — sound, heavy, restful, peaceful sleep. My eyelids are getting heavy — heavy. I am going to close them and go to sleep."

Don't try to count imaginary sheep jumping over fence rails. Don't count numbers. It is a bad habit.

If these suggestions do not help you the first night, say: "All right, my brain was too active; tomorrow I will let down a bit."

Next night eat one or two dry crackers; chew them slowly, masticate them thoroughly until you can swallow easily.

This little food will draw the blood pressure from the brain and help you to go to sleep.

Drive out business and worry thoughts. Think faith and courage thoughts.

40.

To live down the past and erase the errors, live the present boldly.

Do not chastise or condemn yourself for mistakes you have made. You are not alone; everyone has made missteps has hurt others or wronged himself.

Everyone has had reverses and met trouble and misfortune. It's, the plan of things. It is by undergoing trials like these that we **Making** gain in experience and wisdom. We **Mistakes.** are enabled to correct our future acts by utilizing the lessons which our mistakes have taught us.

Yesterday is dead; forget it. Face about. Live today; be busy, be active, be intent on doing right and accomplishing things worth while.

The world's memory is short. A misdeed, an error, a wrongful act on your part may set busy tongues wagging today, and you may suffer from calumny and criticism. Of course, your errors will be magnified and your wrongs enlarged beyond the truth; that's the penalty you pay for your transgressions.

Lies are always added to truth in telling of one's misdeeds. Be brave. Weather the storm; it will soon blow over. Tomorrow the world will forget.

You've suffered in your own conscience; that's all the debt you can pay on the old score.

Now, then, get busy with the glorious opportunity that today presents. Don't make the same mistake again. There are no eyes in the

Worrying Won't Help. back of your head; look forward. Don't worry by envying the other fellow and comparing his good deeds with your mistakes; you only see his good. He has had troubles and made mistakes, too, but you and the world have forgotten them.

If every man's sins were printed on his forehead, the crowds that pass by would all wear their hats over their eyes.

I'm trying to comfort you, and slap you on the back, and tell you that you are just human, and all humans make false steps.

The patriarchs in the Bible made mistakes, but they got in the fold. History has perpetuated their names. Their lives, on the whole, were worth while. It's the sum total of acts that count.

41.

One man says the present is everything, that eternity is nothing. The other man says eternity is everything, that the present is nothing

I believe the real truth is that both are man's chief concern, and neither view **Today and** comprehends all truth. In this **Tomorrow.** matter, the general rule I have so often pointed out will harmoniously apply. That rule is: Avoid extremes.

Those who believe that the Now, the Present, is the all-important thing in man's life have the fashionable or favorite point of view.

Man has much definite information about the present, he knows much about life. He is in the midst of life — it pulsates all around him and in him.

We know positively that the law of compensation is inexorable in its demand for right and positive in its punishment of wrong.

We know that on this earth kindness, love, occupation, help, truth, honor and sympathy are investments which bring happiness today. You get your pay instantly when you have done a helpful act, and you get your punishment instantly when you have done a hurtful act.

That there is a future most of us agree, because good sense and **The Hereafter.** logic point to that sane and reasonable conclusion. So be it. With a belief in the future estate, it is reasonable to assume that our acts and lives in the present will have influence on our future estate.

We know positively of today; we know the happiness we can get from good deeds done today. We come to this knowledge by experience.

If we will have power in the future to look back on today's acts, well and good if today's acts are worth while.

The other view, that Eternity is everything and the present is nothing, is the antiquated view, the narrow view—the, I might say, illiterate view.

That view warps the present life; it calls for present self-chastisement, present gloom, present sorrow and present misery.

It takes the tangible definite today, calls it nothing, and accepts the intangible unknown eternity as everything.

It trades the definite for the indefinite. It calls life a bubble, a vapor, a shadow. In fact, it throws a pall over today's sunshine, and **A Cheerless Philosophy.** reguards our earthly life as a sort of purgatory — a dismal unhappy punishment ante-chamber where man exists and waits, peeping out of his cell windows for a little imagined view of eternity.

He waits and endures the unpleasant interval, steeled against the definite pleasures of today, his whole outlook colored by a fanatical and intoxicated belief in the expected happiness of the undefined future.

He refuses to think of the definite life of today that we all know, and spoils the thought of those who do.

He is a blockade to progress, a disagreeable part of life's picture.

He gets no happiness in the today which is in his hands; he loses his opportunity to be of service here, and lives in the hope of a vague and nebulous future state which has no connection with the realities of every-day life.

Both theories as ultimate beliefs are wrong, yet each has some truth in its conclusion.

By taking the words "Eternity" and "Present" and saying that both mean everything, we avoid extremes and form a truth that is rational, and harmonious to good reason.

The man who says that the present is all, does so because he is an utilitarian. He reasons from the definite and the seeable, and refuses to believe in the abstract. Anything that is outside the sphere of his vision and action is of little concern to him.

The man who says eternity is all, wastes a golden opportunity and warps himself into a miserable hermit.

Life is irrevocable. Every act in our life is placed, set, and fixed.

Every act goes in the record book of yesterday, and it cannot be changed.

Acts that hurt others will rebound and hurt us. Deeds that help others will rebound and help us. This much is certain.

There is a future, I believe that. There is a God, I believe that.

Just what the future is, and just what God is, I do not know in perfect detail.

Reward for good and punishment for evil is part of God's plan, and I am conscious of this truth.

I know that justice prevails in this life, and this life is what I am living now.

If I live and act today in accordance with what I sincerely believe is in tune with God's purpose,

I shall, in my future estate, benefit by those acts. If I live and act today in disregard of all around me, selfishly catering to my personal desires and believing that eternity is everything and the present nothing, I am neglecting the opportunity to do good now in the hope of a **The Good That** future personal reward, the very **Lies At Hand.** nature of which is unknowable. I shall therefore strive to do, and to be, right — to be kind, helpful, cheery and smiling now, for the reward such acts bring now.

And I shall doubtless have as good a record and passport to the future as the man who suffers now and lives only upon his selfish hope of the future.

His is the faith of fear, mine the faith of reason in the all-wise, all-powerful, all-seeing, all-knowing Ruler of the universe, who gave me my life, my brain, my reason, which I am trying to use, as well as my limitations will permit, in helping myself and helping others to smile, to be happy, to be serene, to be confident, to be competent, to be useful.

Everything lives and dies in accordance with the plan of the Creator of the Universe, and you are an atom and I am an atom in that Universe, which is governed by a power too big and great for us to comprehend.

Verily we presume when we say: "We have all the truth; think as we do or you are lost."

The old world has not told its full story. The Universe of which this world is a part is still a deep, unfathomable mystery.

We shall not know all truth until the great revealing time.

The Use of Today. We cannot change the pages of the millions of years gone by. We can do every little to change the pages of the millions of years to come. What little we can do, we can only do TODAY. Today is yours and mine; let's do the best we can with our possession in act and thought and word.

The sun goes down behind the skyline on the West as it has done for millions of years. I lay aside my pen with a bigger view, a deeper appreciation of the Creator, and a profounder faith in His wisdom and works than ever.

God made. God rules. God plans. And verily, we are weaklings and foolish who presume by selfish prayer to suggest to Him what He shall do.

Let us strive to be appreciative of Him; let us try to lift ourselves to the sublime plane of realizing that we are part of Him and His plan, and that failure is impossible to us, if we keep up and on, doing good, speaking softly, dealing gently, showing kindness to-day, and living in accordance with the big, broad, generous, charitable plan instead of in the little, bigoted, narrow, selfish, conceited idea that we are sole possessors of truth and that the man who differs with us in belief is in error.

This chapter is about big things, and in it is a big moral for all who are big enough to grasp it.

42.

"I believe in him because he is so sincere." You've heard that, haven't you? I never could understand how a sensible person could use such logic. Sincerity is no evidence of truth. The Hindu mother is sincere when she throws her babe to the crocodiles, but her **Sincerity and** sincerity is no proof that by this **Truth.** sacrifice she is sure of her salvation.

The Christian Scientist is sincere in the belief that medicines do not cure diseases. The doctor is equally sincere in his belief that medicines do cure disease.

The Theosophist is sincere, the Atheist, the Agnostic, the Christian, the Pagan, the Mohammedan, the Buddhist, the Sunworshipper, the Republican, the Democrat, the Progressive, the Prohibitionist, the Brewer, all these are sincere in their beliefs. And as these beliefs are different, it is common sense to say that no one creed, sect, belief, branch, dogma or system includes or embodies all truth.

It is true that every channel or avenue we meet in life's travel has some truth, but it is not for you or me to assume that we are the **No Monopoly** sole possessors of wisdom and the **On Truth.** real discoverers of all truth. We must not take the conclusions we arrive at and expect to force the world to accept without protest our rules for conduct, our methods for living, our practices for morals, or our beliefs for their guidance.

Converts to new doctrines, new issues, new cults, and to the old ones, too, are made largely because the ambassadors seem so fervid and sincere in expounding what they claim is the definite truth.

The believers in a cult or code of ethics are auto-hypnotized; their visions are narrowed.

By focusing their thought on their special belief, they bring together sophistry, argument, example and so-called proof that gives them facility in arguing the case or expounding their doctrine.

Christian Science.

You can make no gain in trying to argue with a Christian Scientist. You ask for concrete rules, definite answers and proofs other than their flat statements, and you are told you have not the understanding you do not view the subject from the right plane, and that the truth cannot be shown you.

You are told to have faith and belief, to eliminate antagonism, and to study "Science and Health," and you will receive the divine spirit and see the light.

The Scientist is sincere; he shows you "Science and Health " with a lot of testimonials in the back to prove that Christian Science cures disease. Every patent medicine, every science, every system of healing has testimonials by the hundreds.

Scientists say there is no disease, no material that we are only spirit or soul or thought —that we are not matter but mind. Health, they tell us, is truth and disease is error. They deny disease, yet "Science and Health" and the mid-week experience meetings have testimonials of disease cured by Christian Science.

There is much truth in Christian Science. People are helped by it; people are sincere in their belief in it, but that Christian Science is all truth, all-powerful, all-right, all-sufficient, cannot be proven.

What about the people who have gone hence before Christian Science was ever heard of?

The theological religion of to-day differs radically in practice and belief from what it was fifty years ago.

If the Protestant religion be all truth, what became of our religious ancestors who died before Martin Luther found the truth?

I have no quarrel with the Christian Scientist, the Protestant, the Roman Catholic, the Buddhist or the Mohammedan. I must be generous and broad enough to admit that others have the right to think and be sincere. All sciences have truth, but no science, sect, cult, dogma or creed is ALL truth.

The Spirit of Tolerance.

Sincerity is evidence of honest conviction, but that your sincerity in your belief must be accepted by me as proof that I should believe as you do, is, I believe, the place where I have the undoubted right to say: "I reserve the right to my own conclusions, and I would be unjust to myself if I should force myself to accept your viewpoint without fully satisfying myself that you were right."

So, because a person is sincere in a conviction that is contrary to your conscientious belief, do not be disturbed. there is no need to swerve from your own common sense analysis of the matter, or be convinced against your better judgment.

No one possesses all the truth. It is for you and me to do our plain duty as we see it — to do the best we can each day in act and thought and word.

We can pretty much agree on the simple essential truths which are proven. That is—being honest, truthful, kind, lovable, sympathetic, cheerful; doing good, helping one another, and doing things worth while.

If we agree on these things, and do useful work, and think helpful thoughts, we are doing our duty.

Theories, arguments and studying too deeply on bootless systems, codes, beliefs, cults, isms and doctrines, is a waste of time. When we can, here and now, derive definite benefits from doing the simple and **Unprofitable** benefits from doing the simple and **Speculation.** helpful things, and acting and thinking the simple, practical cheer thoughts, it is neither necessary nor helpful for us to waste time on spiritualism or theoretical beliefs that cannot be proven to our own satisfaction.

We are asked to believe these strange, impractical, unnatural beliefs because of the sincerity of others. It's better to believe and to credit the things we can ourselves measure, understand and sincerely adopt.

There are hundreds of strange beliefs and spiritual systems, each claiming to be all-powerful, all-right. If any one is all truth, then all the others are all wrong.

The bigot who assumes he is the sole possessor of truth the cult, sect, ism, or science that claims to possess all truth and presumes to lay down the exact rules for the world to obey — should be classed with those misguided religions and institutions of the dark past which burned human beings who dared to doubt their claim to the possession of all truth and knowledge.

God never gave his approval to any one manmade religious sect.

God is the universal good power. Man often tries to dwarf God's idea to the narrow dimensions of his own small soul.

43.

Whiskey must go. It is written on the pages of the record book of man's progress. Likewise must the quack doctor and the fake medicine go. They

Whiskey and Fake Medicines. have had their day. The quack doctor has already breathed his last in many parts of the country. The fake medicine schemes are still with us, but they are becoming increasingly difficult to put over. That they are doomed to extinction, there can be no doubt.

The side-whiskered advertising doctor who magnifies symptoms and proclaims them to be grave forerunners of awful, debilitating disease, is nothing short of a criminal. He is one of the worst of criminals, because he imposes upon the credulity of the ignorant, excites their fear by means of sensational scarehead advertising, and then when he has finally lured them into his spider-web, fleeces them unmercifully. These char-latans are really more contemptible than any old thief, for the thief does not pretend to be anything else but what he is, while the quack doctor swindles and exploits you under the guise of being your benefactor.

As I have repeatedly explained, illness, feeling "out of sorts," local pains and sickness, unless of the contagious or infectious kind, are largely conditions of the mind.

Most of the temporary ailments are caused by constipation, wrong diet or lack of exercise. The doctor gives a laxative, nature re-asserts herself, and the patient is cured.

Chronic ailments require long treatments — making long bills and many visits for the quack doctor.

Your health and happiness are things largely in your own control. However, when you feel you must have a doctor, go to your **Your Family** family physician and not to a **Physician.** strange physician doctor who advertises. His advertisement is merely a spider web to catch and hold you while he robs you.

It is a hopeful sign of the brighter future toward which man is progressing, that the respectable papers will not lend their aid to swindling doctors. The best papers will not carry these quack doctor or fake medicine ads.

Before long the government will pass laws abolishing this baneful, shameful, quack advertising. Quack doctoring, gambling, liquor selling — these are all swindling methods to get money, and in the getting, the ghouls and parasites who practise these "professions" are killing men, ruining homes, destroying happiness, holding back progress.

The one object of the quack doctor is to size you up and see what you "are good for." "Good for" means how much money can he get from you, and how long can he keep you as a patient to contribute to his coffers.

Let every reader of this book enroll as an opponent to quack doctors and quack medicines, and by word and influence help to hasten the day when such pernicious swindlers and swindling schemes are things of the past.

44.

No two minds can see the same picture in the same way, nor can two persons, armed and equipped with logic, come to the same definite conclusions on religion.

The old Scripture said: "An eye for an eye and a tooth for a tooth." The new Scripture teaches us to "turn the other cheek" and "love our enemies."

Religion, Old and New. Two hundred years ago witchcraft was practised and miserable human beings were burned at the stake. Thirty years ago the preacher who took exception to the universal belief of a hell of fire and brimstone was thrown out of the church. Today no preacher believes in such a hell.

Present day religion is really a Sunday religion. One and a half hours a week the members of the church join in singing, "We shall know each other there." The remainder of the week they make it a point to keep from knowing each other here.

The Protestant church divides itself into numerous sects, each one built on some particular ordinance or practice. Each one, in **Sectarianism** matters of doctrine, will swallow a camel but will strain at a gnat. One sect insists **Sectarianism.** that baptism shall be by immersion because the disciples baptized that way. They believe in following custom literally, yet in the cities they immerse the members in a big tub under the pulpit, which practice is entirely different from the method employed by John the Baptist.

Another sect insists upon having a communion every Sunday because the Bible says, "As often as you do this," etc. To be literal in the matter of communion, the Lord's Supper should be served at night, as the original was, and it should be supper and not a few pieces of broken crackers.

The sect that insists on following the Scriptures in the matter of baptism by immersion fails to follow the Scriptures in the matter of washing the feet or anointing the head.

Many years ago, churches considered it a sacrilege to use an organ. To-day they have orchestras and hire operatic singers.

So it seems that the church is broadening out. Thinking men refuse to believe that religion should any longer be a matter of self-chastisement and worry, sobs and misery. Because so much of this sort of teaching is prevalent, the church is not making the gains it should. The church is largely supported by nice little women many of them maiden ladies who have little to do and know little of the great problems or the busy world.

Live Religion.

I am thoroughly convinced that the church must recognize that a great evolution is taking place — that we must be more charitable, more broad in our views, less technical in our tenets and more practical in our work. We will have to cut down the fences between the sects and get together the great field for a common cause, rather than try to maintain little independent vineyards.

Religion must teach smiles and joy, courage and brotherly love, instead of frowns, dejection. fear and worry.

It must teach us how to be and how to get good out of our today on earth. If we are good and do good here, we certainly need have no fear for our future prospects.

Day by day we are progressing from narrowness, bigotry, selfishness and envy, to broadness reason, brotherly love and contentment, and we **Universal Church.** shall progress from the narrow confines of obstinate orthodoxy or bulidogmatics, by breaking down sect and cult barriers until we are joined together in a universal church in The Universal Church. which all can put their hearts and beliefs — in which all can find full range for their spiritual belief and expression. That big, broad, right church will be in harmony with God's purpose.

The Creator made all men, and He doesn't confine His love or His interest to any one little manmade, narrow sect or creed.

"God is love." "Love thy neighbor." "Help the weak; cheer the grief stricken." Those are the commands and purposes we find everywhere in the Scriptures.

"He that believeth in me shall be saved." That's a definite promise, and it is not qualified by a lot of creed paragraphs and beliefs. That promise doesn't have any "buts" or "ifs." It doesn't say we shall be saved if we be Methodists or Catholics, Baptists or Presbyterians. Those names are manmade, and the creeds of those churches are manmade, too.

At the congress of religions in the World's Fair at Chicago, over three hundred religions and sects were represented by delegates from all over the world, and every one of these delegates, with hearty accord, sang, "Praise God From Whom All Blessings Flow " and"Rock of Ages." Those hymns were universal; they fitted all creeds and sects.

Big men in the church are intensely interested in the get-together universal church, and each year will mark a definite progress toward amalgamation of sects and divisions.

There should be no Methodist Church North and Methodist Church South.

There should not be churches like the Congregational and Presbyterian, whose creeds are identical, the difference being only in the officers.

The country village of 1,000 population has five churches; it should have only one. The country is full of half-starved preachers and weak, struggling congregations.

The get-together movement will help religion, and it's going to happen surely.

45.

Every year the business man goes over his stock, tools, fixtures, and accounts, and prepares a statement of assets and liabilities so as to get a fairly accurate understanding of his profit and loss.

If he didn't take this inventory, his net worth would be a matter of guess work.

Self Inventory. This inventory, which deals with money, materials, etc., and things which are mixed more or less with the human element, is affected by conditions of trade, crops, competition, supply and demand.

The business man takes all these conditions into consideration in preparing for the coming year. He red flags the mistakes and green flags the good plans.

The business man should carry the inventory further. Every month or so he should take a careful inventory of himself, putting down his assets of health, initiative, patience, ability to work, smiles, honesty, sincerity, and the like. So

Listing the Liabilities. also he should put down on the debit side in the list of liabilities the pull-backs, hindrances and other business-killers. These items are un-truth, unfairness, sharp practice, grouchiness, impatience, worry, ill-health, gloom, meanness, broken word, unfilled promises and the like.

In making up the inventory, pay particular attention to your habits: smoking, drinking, overeating, useless display, useless social functions, and other useless things that pull on your nerves and your pocket book.

Then check up department A, which is your family. How have you dealt with your family and children?

Department B is friends. How do you stand in your treatment of them?

Department C includes all other persons. Did you lie to, steal from, cheat or defraud any one? How much cash profit did you make? How much less a man did the act make you?

Go over your self-respect account. Does it show profit or loss?

Check up your employees' account. What has your stewardship shown? Have you drawn the employees closer, or have you driven them further from you?

Balancing the Statement. Analyze your spiritual account. Is your re-ligious belief a sham or a conviction? Do you sing on Sunday, "We shall know each other there," or do you make it a point to know and love your brother here, seven days a week?

Be fair in your inventory. Write down the facts in the two columns designated "good" and "bad," then go over the list and put a red danger flag on the bad.

Keep the list until next inventory and see whether you have made a gain or loss in your net moral standing.

Don't read this and say, "A good idea." Do the thing literally.

Take a clean sheet of paper and write your personal assets and liabilities down in the two columns marked "good" and "bad."

If this inventory doesn't help, then you may call me a false prophet.

I know the plan is a good one. I know it will help you. If it helps you, you will thank me. There can be no harm in trying, because it's a worthwhile thing to test.

The business man who never takes inventory is likely to bump some day.

46.

The ego is in us. It is a good thing to have, but egotism needs the soft pedal when we speak or do things.

Many people are unconscious of their egotism, yet their conversation carries the suggestion, "Even I, who am superior to the herd, would do this or that."

The Personal Pronoun.

For instance, two persons were arguing about the merits of an inexpensive automobile. Parenthetically, I may say that one belonged to the Ford class, and the other to the can't-afford class. A can't-afford snob came to the rescue of the Ford champion by saying, " That's a good car; why, I wouldn't mind owning one of them myself," and he beamed at the party with the consciousness of having settled the matter and removed the stigma from the Ford car.

This egotism often crops out when one shows a group picture in which he appears. He doesn't wait for you to find him; he pokes his arm over your shoulder and says, "That's me."

To each of us, in the very nature of things, the I" is the center of our world. We see things always through our I's.

If we wish to get along without friction, we must remember that the other fellow has his I's also, and when we try to make him see things through out I's, it makes trouble.

Good Breeding.

The hall mark of education, refinement and character, in the broad sense, is the ability to exclude the personal so far as possible from our conversation. And be big enough to grant to others their undoubted right to see and think from their own standpoint.

Argument develops egotism more than almost anything else will.

How often have you convinced another in an argument?

How often have you been convinced in an argument?

The world is big; there are millions of others in it, and our job is a big one if we 'tend pretty well to our own knittin'.

47.

Four hundred and twenty-six years ago Christopher Columbus landed on an island which he thought was India.

Chris was mighty happy as he put his foot on good old Mother Earth, not so much because he had discovered a new way to India, as he thought, but because his foot touched land.

Two days before he landed on San Salvador, his crew pitched into him and threatened to throw him in the sea and turn back with the ship to Spain.

If Chris had shown the white feather, 1492 would not be the date of the first line in the geography, announcing **The Last Step** **Counts.** the "Discovery of America." Chris had perseverance the stuff that makes men successful. He started to find India by sailing westward. He didn't succeed in his purpose, but his deter-mination was rewarded just the same, for he found a new country, and that was worth while.

Before he started, he was promised ten per cent of the revenue from any lands he might discover. Just imagine what that would mean today.

Columbus had perseverance and pep, and his unwavering fidelity to his cause brought him success in his efforts.

The world has improved since 1492, but the percentage of men who would keep everlastingly at it like Columbus did, has not increased, perhaps.

Columbus sailed with three ships, the largest sixty-six feet long. He steered in the direction of the setting sun. His crew was 120 men. None of them were enthusiastic at the start; all of them disgusted, discouraged and ready to mutiny toward the last.

But Christopher kept the ships pointed West, through rain and shine, through drifting, **Keeping** breezeless days and through wild **Everlastingly** stormy nights. He kept on and on **At It.** and on and he brought home the bacon, which, being interpreted, means that success crowned his efforts.

Perseverance and pep when all is said and done, these are the factors without which no great achievement is possible.

It was the mileage made on October 12th, 1492, that counted.

It is the last step in a race that counts.

It is the last stroke on the nail that counts.

The moral is that many a prize has been lost just when it was ready to be plucked.

Perseverance — patience — pluck — pep — these are magic words. They are the "Open Sesame " of modern life. They open the door to opportunity, and will bring you prosperity, peace and plenty.

48.

The man who ridicules everything is on the toboggan slide, and he will end up by becoming an out-and-out grouch.

You and I know men who never have a pleasant word to say of anyone, or a serious commendation of anything.

Ridicule and Humor.

Ridicule and sarcasm are often coated with would-be humor, and are sometimes decked out as puns. By and by, however, this bias toward ridicule and sarcasm gets to be a habit, and the coat of humor becomes threadbare.

Just at this time friends depart, for the grouch phase of the disease has started.

Sarcasm and ridicule are powerful weapons when used adroitly and for good purposes. But when sarcasm and ridicule are used constantly as a means to generate fun, or as vehicles for humor, then the evil commences. The fun disappears; the sting remains.

People will listen to you for awhile if you good-naturedly ridicule a thing, but when you are known to have the habit, that is when friends give you the go-by.

Sarcasm and ridicule wound deeply; they are hot pokers jabbed in quivering flesh.

A Dangerous Weapon.

Don't juggle with ridicule or sarcasm, for people look beneath the veneer nowadays. They remember and repeat the axiom, "There's many a true word spoken in jest." There are so many beautiful things to say, so many kind expressions to utter, so many helpful hints to give, that we should be ashamed to say or do things even jokingly that may hurt another.

When you ridicule a thing or a person, you may ridicule the tender heart of one you should cheer and help.

Ridicule is the negative approach to a subject anyway; the only good it can accomplish is by reflex action or rebound force.

Ridicule is mistakenly conceived, by many, as humor. It is used because it can so easily be employed, in a seemingly clever way, to create a laugh.

Humor of the clean sort is a rare gift. Humor may easily descend to low comedy through the use of ridicule, and often the audience does not differentiate between low comedy and rare humor.

The masses will laugh when the comedian on the stage hits his friend with a club; that sort of fun-making satisfies adults who have children's brains, and people of similar brain-construction will also laugh at jokes which ride on ridicule. But you who read these lines are worthy of better things; that's why you are reading this book. If, in my audience, there are those who have the ridicule habit, I want to arouse you to a better sense of humor than is possible through the employment of ridicule and sarcasm.

I don't want you to descend to the level of the grouch. The slide-down is so easy; the climbing back is so very hard.

Ridicule and sarcasm are cheap, slap-stick methods to produce fun. They leave a sting many times when you are not aware of it.

When fighting whiskey, sin, corruption or organized evil, then use burning ridicule and caustic sarcasm to sizzle and destroy the things that need to be destroyed.

When You Can Go the Limit. Next time you find yourself using ridicule or sarcasm to provoke mirth, remember you are toying with a habit-forming practice that is likely to get the best of you unless you stop and stop now.

A wife is either a partner or an employee. If a partner, she has a right to the fifty-fifty split on profits; if an employee, she is entitled to her wages. A thrifty husband is commendable, but a show-me-what-you-did-with-that-money husband should be punished by being sentenced

Your Wife and Partner. to attend pink teas, afternoon receptions, and to match samples at the dry goods store.

Married folks must be on a partnership basis, or there's sand in the gear box.

Give the wife the check-book; let her pay the bills. Play fair with her; show her what your income is; give her all you can afford and what economic and wise administration warrants. She'll cut the cloth to fit the garment.

When the husband questions every turn, every move, and doles out every cent, the wife feels like a prisoner or a slave. Wives will do good team work when they are broken to double har-ness with their husbands.

Women are generally raised without being required to economize. They have probably been petted and humored, and are used to preening and smoothing their plumage and looking pretty.

It's the female instinct in the human. In the

animal world, the male has the plumage and does the strutting and fascinating; but in the human animal, the female is the bird with the bright plumage.

Fine Feathers.

You can't expect her to know much about the economic side of the home the moment you slip the ring on her finger.

But she'll shop better than her husband if he takes an interest in her shopping and encourages her in the economical administration of the house-hold budget.

She wants a word of appreciation once in a while. She chills under the surveillance and parsimony of an eagle-eyed, meddlesome husband.

She's a sweet bird, and sweet birds and hawks don't nest well together.

Where the hawk and the dove are in the same cage, the feathers will fly.

As I came through the park this morning, I saw a pair of robins who had the right idea. They shared home responsibilities and did fine team work. I think they were mighty happy, too; daddy red breast looked mighty proud as he hustled worms for the family breakfast.

Mama Robin looked down with loving eyes at her hubby, and the little baby robins sang a chorus of joy at the very privilege of living in such a home.

Worry will fly out of the window the moment the husband and wife lay their cards on the table and play the open hand. The moment one or the other keeps a few cards up their sleeve, then worry and trouble come back.

The moral of this is, husbands and wives: live

together, get together, stay together, play together, save together, grow together, share together. Travel the same road; don't take different paths.

50.

Tonight I am in the Ozarks, and old Mother Earth is passing through the belt of meteoric dust — that great mysterious sea in the universe through which we pass every year about the middle of November.

I look out into the night and marvel at the countless stars in the infinite black void, and wonder how closely those stars may be connected with humanity.

The Stars. That they are connected, I have no doubt, for truly, "the sun, the moon, the stars, and endless space as well, are parts, are things, like me, that cometh from and runneth by one grand power of which I am in truth a part, an atom though I be."

How many stars are there? Well, let's get ready to appreciate number. I can see about 3,000; with opera glasses I could see 30,000.

Franklin Adams some years ago photographed the whole canopy with 206 exposures. He counted the stars by mathematical plans, and published his finding that there were 1,600,000,000 stars.

That number is just about the number of humans on this earth. So, then, there is one star for each of us.

Each of those stars, practically speaking, is larger than the earth. It is thought that many of them may have human beings who think and reason like we do.

Finite and Infinite. Multiply the 1,600,000,000 population on this earth by any portion of the 1,600,000,000 stars that may have thinking creatures on them; multiply that total by the millions of years and millions of generations that have passed out of existence.

Think of these numbers and limitless boundaries, and then tell me, if you can, that one little man on one little star we call Earth has a strangle-hold on truth, and that his viewpoint, his ism, his little dogma, his narrow creed, is all-sufficient, all-right, all-inclusive.

Verily, little protoplasm, you have another guess. We can, by experience and tests, prove two and two make four. We can by practice and experience prove that love, kindness, help, gentleness, sympathy, cheer and courage bring happiness.

These are tangible things that fall within the province of human experience. But when one wee Willie with sober face tells you and me and others that he has the truth about **The Sense of Proportion.** the definite, full workings of God's plans and purposes, I think of the greatness of 1,600,000,000 stars, each with 1,600,000,000 humans, and of the unnumbered generations gone by, and say that verily, we must live TODAY and do the best we can today in act and thought and word.

Yesterday is dead; to-morrow is unknown. Where we have been, where we will be, we know not. Where we are today, we know, and only God in His omniscience knows the final answer as to our future estate.

He will take us and hold us and place us in His keeping and according to His purpose, even though we do not or cannot follow or believe any one of the little man-formed creeds, isms or cults as the measure and rule for our beliefs.

Those stars testify to the certainty of God, and I believe in Him.

51.

When a man by his brains, or by a fortunate combination of circumstances, rises to a position of prominence, he becomes a target for the envious and a pattern for the imitator. Emulation and envy are ever alert in trying **Success** to steal the fruits of the leader or **and Envy.** the doer of things.

The man who makes a name gets both reward and punishment. The reward is his satisfaction in being a producer, a help to the world, and the glory that comes from widespread recognition and publicity of his accomplishment. The punishment is the slurs, the enmity, the envy and the detraction, to say nothing of the downright lies which are told about him.

When a man writes a great book, builds a great machine, discovers a great truth or invents a useful article, he becomes a target for the envious many.

If he does a mediocre thing, he is unnoticed; if his work is a masterpiece, jealousy wags its tongue and untruth uses its sting.

Wagner was jeered. Whistler was called a mere charlatan. Langley was pronounced crazy. Fulton and Stephenson were pitied. Columbus faced mutiny on his ship on the very eve of his discovery of land. Millet starved in his attic. Time has passed, and the backbiters are all in unmarked graves. The world, until the end of time, will enjoy Wagner's music. Whistler and Millet's paintings attract artists from all over the world, and inventors reverence the names of

Fulton and Stephenson.

The leader is assailed because he has done a thing worth while; the slanderers are trying to equal his feat, but their imitations serve to prove his greatness. Because jealous **The Price of** ones cannot equal the leader, they **Greatness.** seek to belittle him. But the truly worth-while man wins his laurels and he remains a leader. He has made his genius count, and has given the creature of his brain and imagination to the world.

Above the clamor and noise, above the din of the rocks thrown at him, his masterpiece and his fame endure.

And compensation, the salve to the sore, makes the great man deaf to the noise and immune to the attacks of the knockers.

In his own heart he knows he has done a thing worth while; his own conscience is clear, and he cares not for the estimate of the world.

His own character is his chief concern, and he is content in the knowledge that time will bring its reward.

If you have high ideals in business, if you achieve success on a big scale, mark well, you will be a subject of attacks, of lies, of malice, of envy, of disreputable competition. There is no way out of it.

But you will be repaid. The lover of fair play, the grateful, true, honest, worth-**Compensation.** while people will flock to your standard; the riff-raff will skulk behind bushes and throw rocks and mud, but their acts will prove to the great mass of the people that your purposes, practices and policies are right.

Therefore, courage is to be your chief asset; patience, pride, perseverance, your lieutenants.

Be not weary, grow not discouraged when your progress is hampered by obstacles. Every truly great man of the past has had his backbiters and detractors.

52.

There are three periods in our lives: the youthful, or prospective period, the adult, or introspective period, and the old age, or retrospective period.

Too many there are who look forward to old age with fear or dread. But old age has its joys and pleasures as well as middle age and youth, and these pleasures are the keener if the first and second periods of life were lived sanely, worthily and properly. Numerous are the great men of the past who have extolled the old-age period of human life with its wisdom and wealth of worldly experience.

Growing Old.

If the middle period is spent in getting dollars only, then old age will be days of empty nothingness.

Youth is the planning time the time for ideals and ambitions; middle age the building time, and old age the dividend time.

With many, old age is spent in reading the book of the past — with sadness as the reader recognizes that the ideals, plans and hopes were shattered. As age turns the page in the book of the past, he reads one hope after another van-ished in smoke.

Anticipation is seldom realized, and this is as it should be, for in time, men will learn to live each day for each day's good and each day's happiness.

Let us perform our duty to-day; let us lay away a kindly act, a smile, a word of cheer in the bank of good deeds.

Each of us has a share in this world's work. It matters little whether our actual share is what we had guessed or wished it to be.

Vicissitudes will cross our path here and there; so-called misfortune or bad luck will strike us **The Value of Ideals.** when least expected. The failure of our dreams should not grieve us. We cannot reach up and grasp the stars, but like the pilot at the wheel at sea, we can steer by those stars that help us on our way.

Our ideal may not be realized, but the journey to it may still be a pleasant one.

Our ideals, plans and hopes had a real purpose, a real service; they gave us courage and made us work, and thus they were well worth while.

We must not, in the old age period, condemn ourselves because our plans failed or our castles were shattered.

There is no hard luck except incurable disease or death. It is not for us to mourn the past or weep for the flowers that are gone.

In our active days, we should realize that we are putting memories away in our brains that will come back to us in old age.

Only that which we put in our brains can we take out.

So then, Mr. Avarice, I warn you: If gold is your God, it's cold comfort you will get in your sunset days.

Build up loving ties, appreciation and the worth-while riches of good deeds, and in your evening of life, you will be welcome wherever you go.

If your life was sold for gold, your evening of life will be short and miserable; legatees will will endure you simply because they grudge you your every breath; they are checking off the days from Time's calendar until the day of your passing, and the dollars you sold your soul and heart and life for, will be lavishly spent by cold-blooded heirs who cared nothing for you.

Put Not Your Faith in Gold.

Leave a legacy of love, example and character, and if, with these, there are a few dollars, they simply prove your frugality, economy and independence.

A few dollars left to heirs will help. Many dollars will hurt. Dollars in old age will give you pleasure by helping in tight corners. They will enable you to help your loved ones over the bumps in the road.

Use the dollars to help those you love to help themselves, and your old age will be a busy, happy one, and you won't be in the way.

To prepare for that happy period of your life, the foundation must be built in the active today period.

Carry smiles into your old age; they will keep the heart young, the digestion good, and life will be worth while.

53.

I have traveled horseback over the great arid plains of the West, and have read the story of the ages gone before.

The Remote Past. In Arizona and New Mexico there are ancient ruins of forts and cities built by people we know not of. Chalcedony Park with its petrified forest of mammoth trees silently testifies to a period when vegetation was rampant on what is now a desert.

In Wyoming there is coal enough to furnish fuel for the United States for several centuries.

Coal is carbon made from decayed trees and vegetation, which became covered with earth and rock, and was subjected to tremendous pressure throughout the thousands of years required to effect the transformation.

Oceans and floods gradually covered millions of acres of trees and plants with ooze and soil and sand. Ages turned some of these deposits to stone.

There in bleak Wyoming is testimony and evidence of changes that time only can bring about.

"A thousand years is as a day and a day is as a thousand years." Thus wrote the scribe of old. So, then, we must consider this estimate of time in reading the first chapter of Genesis which describes the order of the world's creation.

First took place the dividing of light from darkness, thus bringing about the rotation of day and then, the separating of land and water; then, the birth of vegetation on the land, the creation of fish and reptiles in the sea, the fowls of the air, the beasts of the field, and finally, the higher animal, man.

The pages of the earth's surface carry in their stratification indelible records harmonizing with this scriptural account of the evolution of the earth from its chaotic misty past to its concrete definite present. Yes, this earth of ours is old, so old that mere man cannot contemplate or accurately estimate its wondrous age.

The fossils of the mammoth reptiles and beasts which lived before the appearance of man on this planet are numerous in the fascinating West I know so well.

In those arid desert hills are bones of the ancient rhinoceros — parent of our horse — and there are shells, and fossils of fish, and bones of animals imbedded in the strata of rock.

Man reads these pages and he is lost in bewilderment, impoverished in thought, dumb for words, paralyzed by his inability to co-ordinate this evidence with any measure of time that will fall within the range of human comprehension.

The Age of The Earth.

Historians say the world was 4,004 years old before the Christian era, and 1918 years have passed since then, making the age to date 5,922 years. It is not surprising that through the dark ages, dates and facts were lost. We have not a complete history in written language, but we have some very definite history in the rocks and hills and lands and seas.

The world certainly is more than 5,922 years old. Read the record of time so plainly visible at Niagara Falls.

Niagara Falls eats away about two feet of rock in a century; the gorge is a good many miles long. At the present rate of erosion, it takes 2,640 years to eat away a mile. Multiply that by the distance between the falls and Lake Ontario and you have an idea of how many years Niagara Falls has been at work.

Before Niagara Falls was in existence, the country round about was under the sea; before that, under glaciers; before that, in the tropics, and I don't know how many times it has swung on its pendulum between Frigid, Temperate and Torrid Zones.

We are certain to become lost in a labyrinth of mystery when we take these known facts concerning the earth's age, and try to specify any particular number of millions of years as the old world's age.

54.

And now my pleasant occupation of writing this book draws to an end. I sincerely hope you have received some definite suggestions that will be helpful to you.

To get you to think — that has been my aim. To get you to analyze yourself — to take stock of yourself — to know yourself — that has been the task I set before me.

Think vital thoughts of courage, faith and hope.

Then will your days pass joyfully, and your path be one of peace, happiness and contentment. If you fill your mind with gloom and sorrow thoughts, your surroundings will reflect your mental attitude and will accentuate your misery and dejection. Do not give **How to Think.** way to this weak, gloomy, pernicious thinking. You can be strong, you will be strong if you learn to control your thought habits.

Can you face disagreeable facts without wavering? Can you meet adversity with courage in your heart and a smile on your lips? You can, if you have read this book carefully, calmly, thoughtfully, and put into practice the rules I have laid down.

Do not think that you can go through life without your share of pain, disillusion and disappointment. It can't be done. No man has ever done it. Clouds will come, but they can be dispelled. Obstacles will arise, but they can be surmounted. Troubles will visit you, but meet them boldly and courageously and do not show the white feather.

To the thinking man or woman, life is a great arena wherein good and bad, joy and sorrow, faith and disillusion, happiness and unhappiness, success and failure are inextricably intermingled. The joy and happiness, accept gratefully; the sorrow and disillusion, bear with fortitude. And remember, although it is not possible to enjoy an absolute and continued state of happiness, it always lies within your power to have serenity, poise, peace and contentment.

When you are in the dumps — when that feeling of the hopelessness and un-worthwhileness of life comes over you, then, more than ever, think. Do not give way to fear and despondency. Think cheerful thoughts; think of the good things that life has given you, not the least of them being life itself. Think of the ringing words that Milton put into the mouth of Lucifer, the fallen angel, in "Paradise Lost":

"The mind is its own place, and in itself Can make a heaven of hell, a hell of heaven."

To the person who thinks, life is ever-new, ever-interesting. If you have lost your grip on reality — if you have dwelt too long in the shadowland of doubt, fear and despondency — the thing to do is to correct your thinking. **Life's Ever-New Newness.** Let your mind soar in contemplation of the beautiful things of nature. Steel yourself against petty pullbacks and recognize them for what they really are — trifling annoyances that serve no purpose except to distract you from the pursuit of the great and glorious goal that lies ahead.

Only to the thinking man is it given to see life and see it whole. He only has the true sense of

171

proportion. He keeps his eye on the main objective, secure in the realization that he is master of himself and captain of his own soul. He is self-sufficient, for he knows that no matter what befalls, he carries happiness and contentment within himself wherever he goes.

The practice of thinking is a tower of strength. If you are a thinker, life's little troubles serve but to reinforce your spirit of resistance and make you stronger.

So then, let this be my last word to you — think! — for it is by thinking that man has risen to his present high estate in the world. It is by thinking that the future joy and happiness and peace of the world must be increased.

Chip Eichelberger, CSP

Chip Eichelberger gets his audiences to say
WOW! His **action** on stage translates to
excitement in the audience, and his customized
keynotes and seminars produce **results** for every
meeting. He entertains with his natural **humor**
and a relevant message that consistently
captivates audiences.

Formally Tony Robbins international point-
man, Chip can **challenge, enlighten,** and
motivate. Meeting planners find his accessibility
and attention to detail refreshing. Chip does not
do a one-way keynote address, but creates an
interactive experience. If he opens or closes
your meeting, your event goes from **good to
great!** *His accessibility, adaptability and
wonderful attention to detail are the attributes
you need in a professional speaker.*

If you like energy, humor, spontaneity, and
simple-to-implement strategies that you can use
at once, then *Chip Eichelberger* is for you. His
electrifying speaking style, finely honed on three
continents and in nine countries, gives him a rare
ability to challenge, enlighten and motivate. He
will entertain you with a natural humor and a
relevant message that consistently captivates his
audiences. You will find his accessibility,
adaptability, and wonderful attention to detail
refreshing. *Chip does not do a "one-way"
keynote address, he creates an interactive
experience.*

Chip has an incredible track record of getting
measurable results for companies and getting
audiences to say "WOW"! Ask anyone who has
seen him live. For the past nineteen years, Chip

has been an achiever in the only place that counts — the trenches. After earning his BS from the University of Oregon, Chip was an award winning salesperson for Jantzen Sportswear. In 1988 he joined world famous author and motivator *Anthony Robbins* and quickly became the top field sales leader and trainer in his six years there.

Check out his web site at GetSwitchedOn for information on his best selling products.

Gaining the Edge! – 6 CD Series – $49.95
It's Not What the Market is Doing,
What are You Doing?– Double CD – $24.95
Get Switched On! DVD – $34.95

He pioneered new markets in the United Kingdom and Australia for the Robbins organization as the principal international point man before launching his solo career. Chip has a magical ability to generate **enthusiasm,** contagious **energy,** and **results** that will last well beyond his program. Your audience will be energized to begin their time focused and inspired to get the most out of their time together or leave with the inspiration to implement a specific game plan to take action on.

Chip did over 1300 talks while with Anthony Robbins before collecting his first speaking fee. What does that mean to you? He has paid his dues perfecting his skills and gives an exceptional performance every time. He will make you look good and be an **indispensable part** of your successful event!

Clients include: Bank of America, Prudential, State Farm, IBM, Sun Microsystems, American Dental Association, Procter & Gamble, Glaxo SmithKline, Castrol, PriceWaterhouseCoopers, American Standard, Culligan, Toyota, Ford, Lincoln Mercury, Century 21, Bechtel, BellSouth, Cingular, SkyTel, Eckerd, CVS, Washington Hospital Center and the Association of Operating Room Nurses.

"You surpassed all expectations and help lead Terminix to one of the most successful jumpstarts to the year we have experienced. No speaker has ever spent the time in the field learning our sales structure and business like you did."
Terminix, Bill Sublette, VP of Sales

"WOW! We knew you were going to be good, but quite honestly, **you bring new meaning to the concept of exceeding expectations.** Your ability to transfer enthusiasm, while incorporating your message with the vision of our company, really hit home for our management team."
Safeway, Greg Sparks, President

"The effort that you put forth in preparing for the presentation was evident. Your message was on target, exciting, motivating and relevant."
Meineke, Gene Zhiss, VP of Marketing

"Your message was simply inspirational, believable, humorous and most importantly sincere. I received countless comments on not only how energized they felt, but also how

amazed they were that an "outside speaker" could leave everyone with the impression you were a long-term employee."
Boston Scientific, David Bee,
Director Program Management

*Chip is a **Certified Speaking Professional.** The CSP designation is the highest earned designation awarded by the National Speakers Association to recognize proven expertise and experience. Fewer than 7% of the speakers worldwide have earned this prestigious designation.*

Chip Eichelberger
865-717-1155
GetSwitchedOn.com
Chip@GetSwitchedOn.com